Peer to Peer Lending

How to Get Your Peer-to-peer Investments Started

(How the World's Largest Peer to Peer Lender Is Transforming Finance)

Brian Webb

Published By **Darby Connor**

Brian Webb

Peer to Peer Lending: How to Get Your Peer-to-peer Investments Started (How the World's Largest Peer to Peer Lender Is Transforming Finance)

ISBN 978-1-77485-668-0

Legal & Disclaimer

The information contained in this ebook is not designed to replace or take the place of any form of medicine or professional medical advice. The information in this ebook has been provided for educational & entertainment purposes only.

The information contained in this book has been compiled from sources deemed reliable, and it is accurate to the best of the Author's knowledge; however, the Author cannot guarantee its accuracy and validity and cannot be held liable for any errors or omissions. Changes are periodically made to this book. You must consult your doctor or get professional medical advice before using any of the suggested remedies, techniques, or information in this book.

Upon using the information contained in this book, you agree to hold harmless the Author from and against any damages, costs, and expenses, including any legal fees potentially resulting from the application of any of the information provided by this guide. This disclaimer applies to any damages or injury caused by the use and application, whether directly or indirectly, of any advice or information presented, whether for breach of contract, tort, negligence, personal injury, criminal intent, or under any other cause of action.

You agree to accept all risks of using the information presented inside this book. You need to consult a professional medical practitioner in order to ensure you are both able and healthy enough to participate in this program.

TABLE OF CONTENTS

Introduction

Peer-to-peer lending is a new and exciting investment opportunity that you could take advantage of and earn lots of money! Apart from letting you earn passive income, peer-to-peer lending can also be an innovative, flexible and diverse method of investing your funds.

This guide offers expert advice to help you gain knowledge before you decide to consider peer-to peer lending as a profitable investment opportunity. Learn the fundamentals of peer-to peer lending, learn the techniques to remain secure when trading online Diversify your investment portfolio and reap attractive returns.

It is also crucial to remember that, just like all types of investing, peer-to peer lending can be risky when it comes to your money. This book will help you to learn more for reducing the risk of your investment and be successful in your investment endeavors.

Thank you to buying this book. I hope you enjoy it!

Chapter 1: An Introduction To Peer-To-Peer Lending

"Be your own Bank...Not you, the banker."

When I read these words in Robert Kiyosaki's Rich Dad's Cash flow Quadrant Rich Dad's Guide for Financial Freedom, Part 2 the whole thing began to click.

I thought to myself "How do I borrow money and make it be useful instead of working to earn it?"

Kiyosaki states the reason why one of his most popular investment options is to buy the property and then sell it while holding an interest on the loan for the buyers, effectively creating a bank since, like the bank, he is paid on a monthly basis and also earns interest, and the note is listed as an asset in the balance account.

In the past 12 years, I've been fascinated by investments that let me loan money and build my wealth in methods other than investing in stocks. It's not a bad thing I think it's crucial to be a part of stocks, however I am not a fan of the constant fluctuations within my investment portfolio. and prefer investing in assets that simply rise, don't?

Robert Kiyosaki and many other investors don't have any problem purchasing the five or six figure asset in cash and then selling it after securing the mortgage. For me, I'd rather invest in smaller amounts and create an array of more diverse notes rather than worrying about what could happen if one of my properties ran into trouble. A larger collection of loans and smaller notes makes me more comfortable at night.

Since I read those words in 1998, I've made small (less than 5 figures) loans, mostly to finance mobile home purchases and tax lien certificates. However in 2010 I read an article that discussed the growing popularity of Peer-to -Peer Lending. I acted upon reading that article. In this book, I'll discuss with you two years of learnings that helped me develop winning strategies and secure return on these loans.

What is Peer-to–Peer Lending?

Peer-to peer (P2P) lending or also known as Person-to-Person lending happens when a person gets the loan of several people. Peer-to-Peer lending is a phenomenon that has been around for Think about the number of times you've borrowed money from your friendor given someone $1.00 to drink, but on a smaller scale, you've made an individual-to-person loan. There is no bank involved since you're acting as a bank. Moreover, If you had wanted to, charge interest, you might have, and even earned money through the lending.

Why should you not take a loan from the bank?

P2P lending is beneficial for borrowers as they can eliminate intermediaries (the banks) and reduce the interest they pay. In the case of P2P, someone with a great FICO(r) score (credit) rating and a low debt-to-income ratio can get rates that is as low as 6.75 percent for what amounts to a signature loan , whereas the lowest rate I can find at the credit union I work at for this kind of credit is 10.15 percent. Thus, a borrower with a good credit score can easily save more than 3percent of the interest they pay each calendar year for their loans.

The bank's elimination can be beneficial to investors. Instead of letting the bank earn 10% of their profits and only pay .6 percent, you'll be able increase the amount you earn by 10 times the amount. This book will provide the information and the information you require to earn more and still be able to sleep. This book will assist you create a strong portfolio of loans, and you will earn an excellent ROI from your investments.

The Borrowing Process

Before you invest in anything it is important to understand how it works. in this article we'll examine how borrowing works and the way one can apply for a peer-to-peer loan.

Step 1. The borrower (the person in need of an loan) submits a loan application through the P2P website. The loan ranges anywhere from $1000 to $35,000, and are available to be used for anything from debt consolidation to weddings and holidays. The borrower will fill out an application for loan. During the process of applying for the loan they must give information about their earnings, employment status and what they intend to utilize the loan proceeds for and their personal details like Social Security Number, and other vital information. It's the same information you'd give to a bank if you apply for loans.

Step 2: After the application has been submitted After that, the P2P Lending site will confirm the information provided and will obtain the details of the bank account used by the borrower which will be used to transfer the proceeds and to collect the monthly installments. The loan is listed under "Approved" Condition. That means that the borrower has proved who they are as well as that the company has verified the information and that it is in compliance with the requirements for lending that are set by the website. This is also a sign that loan can be approved only if and only if it convinces investors to sponsor the loan, and then ultimately finance the loan.

Step 3. The loan is placed on the site for review by loan buyers (you along with me). The loan is open to review for 14 days. The loan is approved if investors agree to provide at 60 percent of the amount requested before the end of the 14-day listing period.

Step 4: After you have confirmed that the P2P site has verified the bank account information, has received the loan paperwork signed and confirmed the loan The requested funds including a loan origination fee is transferred directly to the borrower's bank account.

5. The loan is registered on the credit report of the borrower, which means it is an obligation that is current and any collection or late payments are also noted. As opposed to taking money out from a relative it is a genuine credit obligation with real consequences if the borrower fails to pay, it's listed on their credit report , and it will impact their score on credit.

Step 6: Every loan is automatically collected through money transfer from the bank account of the borrower on the due date , and afterward, the loan payments are distributed to investors on a pro-rata basis. If you've invested 1percent of the loan amount you'll get one percent of the monthly payments. I'll go over the details in a future post.

The Investing Process

After the loan has been through the initial approval process and is uploaded on the website investors will then begin to look over the loan paperwork and identify loans that are in line with our requirements for loan and can determine how much we're willing to put in the loan. The site which I have used, investment are required to be made within multiples of $25.00 The minimum amount that you can invest in a loan is $25.

During the review process you are able to inquire about the lender. The Lending Club site, you are able to only ask questions that have been approved by the lender for example:

* What is the intended application of the proceeds of your loan?

How much are you spending on your monthly costs (rent or transportation, utilities telephone food, insurance, etc.)?

• What is your month-long costs in connection with the housing (rent, mortgage(s), home equity loans and / (or line of credit and/or line of credit, taxes, utilities, insurance and so on)?

* If you've experienced an unpaid debt in the past two years, please give the reason.

* Please describe the reason for why you have the large balance of your revolving credit.

In the event that you hold a record of a public nature in your file, please describe the incident and the resolution.

* If you're in the process of paying for a mortgage, you must breakdown all of your costs associated with your housing (mortgage payment and insurance, taxes and so on).

* If you're using your loan to fund multiple purposes What are the goals and how do you allocate the funds?

* What debts do you intend to settle with this loan?

What do you have in your current debt balances as well as interest rates and monthly payments based on the type (credit cards and mortgages, student loans credit lines, etc.)?

You don't get to look at!

The loan documents will give you many valuable details about the borrower. However, it does not divulge any personal details about the borrower, like their address, name telephone number, address, as well as their social security. Figure 1 is an example the loan documentation taken from Lending Club. If this were a loan that you were looking to invest then you'd make it available for purchase after which, once the loan was approved, you will begin receiving part of your monthly payments.

Image 1: Loan Information

How do I get paid?

Every month, as the money is withdrawn from the account of the borrower You will be able to get your share of the amount. Take a examine the following example to learn more about how payments are divided. In this instance, we'll take the data from the loan documents in Figure 1.

If I put up $25 to get this loan of $12,000 I would have .2083 percent of the loan. Therefore, my share of each monthly installment will be $.77 each month.

When the funds are received, each investor will be assessed a service fee of 1percent of the total amount paid to compensate for the payment to P2P Lending site for their service of credit (collection as well as processing the monthly installment). The effect on my account will be less than one cent, which is not evident.

So on a monthly basis, my bank account is charged to $.76 due to this loan. When the loan comes not paid on time during a particular month, then the borrower will be penalized with a late fee of $15 and the late charge is divided in an equitable basis to the investors who took this note. So in this instance, my share will be an additional $.03 every month.

To determine exactly what your part of your monthly payment will be, make use of a financial calculator or a site for payment calculators for a better one:

Calculator for Bank Rates

The 76 cents is Chump Change

In the previous example I've made use of an investment minimum of $25.00 since I would like you to realize that you don't need to be a complete beginner when investing in this kind of investment. If you are more confident investing of $250, then the net monthly installment would be $7.60. If you're assured, you can pay for the entire loan or any part in between It all depends on the amount of capital you're willing to invest and how confident you are with the decision and the ability of the borrower to repay you.

Who are the top P2P Lending Sites?

There are two primary websites within the P2P market, LendingClub.com and Prosper.com. Both sites have similar offerings in terms of the products they provide, but they each have their own method of determining the interest rate that a borrower pays and we'll discuss more in the next chapter.

Chapter 2: How Interest Rates Are Calculated

The most significant distinction between the two major P2P lending platforms is the way they decide what rate of interest that a borrower has to pay and, consequently, the interest rates that investors can earn. In the case of Lending Club, the interest rate is calculated using several factors exactly as it would have been if the borrower were to the bank. The greater the risk, the greater the amount of interest the loan will earn. On Prosper.com They also employ an algorithm to calculate the interest rate. However, investors can also negotiate the interest rate lower which results in a lower price for the lender but potential lower returns for the investor. Based on my experiences, Lending Club offers a higher return for investors from an investment viewpoint and will continue to do so from now on we will be focusing specifically on Lending Club investing, even that the principles discussed in the book can be applied to both platforms.

Assessing Risk

Lending Club uses the following formula to calculate the interest rate for a borrower:

Lending Club Base Rate plus Adjustment to Volatility and Risk

The formula, the Base Rate is regularly adjusted according to the latest rates of interest. At the moment of writing Base Rate is 5.05 percent, and the adjustment for Volatility and Risk is based upon a range of elements, such as:

* The loan amount you are requesting

* The amount of credit inquiries made in recent times.

* The credit history of the borrower's length

* The current and total balance of open credit accounts.

* The credit utilization that is revolving.

* The loan's requested maturity is either 36 months or 60.

Every loan is subject to an 8-step process in order in order to decide what the appropriate adjustment in risk or volatility will be and based on that results, every loan is placed in a sub-group, which determines the final rate of interest Table 1 lists the sub-groups as well as the current interest rates.

To decide what the final percentage of the interest must be evaluated using the following eight steps. Lending Club handles all of the calculations, but I believe it's essential to know the process of calculating interest rates to be able to evaluate the request for loan. To help you understand how this process works I've made an imaginary profile of two borrower; let me show you Jack as well as Jill.

Table 1 - Rates of Interest

In the above chart you can be able to see the financial data which was retrieved out of Jack as well as Jill's credit reports as well as their loan application. The information is utilized to approve their loan and determine their loan's interest rate. Note it is that Jill has a higher FICO(r) Rating than Jack which it appears that she is at a lower chance of being a risk for Jack.

Step 1. the Score of the Borrower's FICO(r) Score

The formula used to calculate the FICO(r) score is not public and as secret as the formula used by Coca Cola, however, Fair Isaacs, the company behind FICO is able to consider the following aspects in calculating the credit score of an individual:

* Pay History (35 percent Weight)

* The Credit Utilization Rate and the Total Debt (30% weight)

* Length of Credit History (15 percent weight)

* Recent inquiries: Number of (10 percent Weight)

With the person's FICO score and the graph below, it's possible to determine the likelihood that he could be up to 90 days behind on a due date in 2 years.

This chart reveals that someone who has 700 points has a chance of 5% of being more than 90 days in late payment within the next two years. If you know what is the FICO(r) score is, and how it can be interpreted Let's take a look at the way Lending Club uses this data.

Everything begins at an initial FICO(r) score that the borrower has. Lending Club uses

Table 2 to determine the sub-group that will be the primary for the loan.

As Jack's FICO(r) Score is 714, it puts him first into the A5 Loan Grade and, because Jill's FICO(r) Score is 725, this places her into the A4 Loan Grade. From the beginning we can see that Jill's score is higher than Jack's.

Table 2: Initial Sub-Grade of Loan

If a borrower's FICO(r) Score lower than 660, the loan application will be rejected.

Step 2: What does the borrower want to borrow?

In Table 3 you'll find the highest recommended guidelines for loans in the guidelines that Lending Club recommends for each borrower based upon the FICO(r) Score. Therefore, those who are initially the subgrade of A1 (FICO(r) score of 780+) is able to apply for up to $35,000 without having to worry about a reduction in their sub-grade. On the other hand, those who are under the sub-grade of C (FICO(r) score of 660 to 678) is able to request up to $12,500 without reduction in their sub-grade.

Table 3 Table 3 Max Loan Guiding Limit

Table 3 will be utilized to alter the sub-grade in accordance with the amount of a loan the borrower wants.

In our case, Jack is requesting $7,000 Table 3 gives the guideline limit of $15,000 this means that Jack is asking less than the limit of guidance and we must consult Table 4 to assess the impact of the loan. To calculate this, we need to divide the amount demanded by the limit of guidance (7,000/15,000 = 46 percent) This means that Jack wants to get 46 percent of the limit of guidance. Table 4 shows the risk modifier of Jack for the amount of loan is 0 which means he is in the same sub-group A5.

Jill however has requested $30,000 and Table 3 gives us the guidance limit of

$20,000 and we must check the percentage of the amount she is requesting for her loan is. 30,000 x 20000 = 150%, looking back at Table 4 it states that Jill currently has an risk-modifier of -6. This implies that she has moved down six sub-grades, which is B5.

Tab 4: Risk Modifier, based on the Loan Size

Therefore, even while Jill has a higher FICO(r) score, at the second stage, her loan is seen as more risky than Jack's because he has less credit score.

Step 3 - The number of credit inquiries

The next stage looks at the amount of times the borrower applied for an installment loan within the past six months. The more times a person tried to obtain an loan or a line of credit the more riskier the loan is because it indicates that the borrower is in need of funds to support their needs. Table 5 lists the risk factors for the amount of credit inquiries over the past six months.

In our instance, Jack had 2 credit inquiries, whereas Jill had none. In Table 5, we can see that the risk factor of Jack is 0 meaning that Jack is still an A5. As Jill did not have any enquiries and her score originally an A4, her Risk Modifier is +1,, which implies she is actually moving into a sub-group that is B4.

Table 5: Risk Modifier for Credit Inquires

Step 4 - Length of Credit in Months

Table 6 illustrates the benefits of having a good credit history. The borrowers with less than 5 years of credit history may be at higher risk than those who have more credit history.

In our example the two Jack as well as Jill have credit histories more than 60 months. Jack has 187 months and Jill has 66, this gives an increase in risk of zero points, which means that Jack is in the A5 and Jill is in the B4 sub-group.

The Risk Modifier Table in the 6th column for Credit History

Step 5 - Number of Accounts Open Accounts

In this stage we will look at the amount of open accounts. This is based on information on the borrower's credit file. In Table 7, you'll see that the open accounts ranging from 6 to 21 do not affect the credit score for the loan. Any less than that is a sign of a borrower with a short time to pay several credit lines. Anything greater than 22, suggests that the loan may be over-extended.

As Jack has five opened lines, his risk factor is -1. This means that his sub-group is dropped from an A5 level to a B1. However, since Jill is open to 12 lines. Her risk modifier stays identical, while her subgroup is still B4.

The amount of open accounts that appear on credit reports might be confusing. Open credit lines do not only include the amount that a person is obligated to pay; they also include accounts that they are authorized to. For instance, if, for example, my wife holds an American Express Card and she adds me as an authorized user it will appear to be an active account in my credit file however, I could not have financial liability for the amount except if it's shared account. It is therefore possible for a borrower's credit score to be affected if they are able to access another's card.

Tab 7: Risk Modifier based on the number of accounts

Step 6 - Revolving Credit Utilization

This is an important figure that tells you whether the person who is borrowing is dependent too heavily on credit cards.

This number is determined by how much available credit is utilized against. how much credit is available for the credit card. If the borrower holds five credit cards that have an aggregate credit line of 10,000 and the current balance of the cards is $9, the revolving credit utilization of his account is 90 percent, which is extremely high. This could indicate that the borrower has leveraged very heavily on their credit cards . This could indicate a root cause.

In the same vein as Jack continuing with Jack Jill In the case of Jack, his utilization is 25.2 percent, and Jill's usage is 54.9 percent. Table 8 shows the risk adjustment for their credit utilization revolving. Both fall in the sweet spot between 5percent - 84.99 percent and both have a risk-modifier of 0. Jack remains a B1 while Jill is a B4.

Tab 8 Risk Modifier for Credit Utilization

Step 7 - The Loan Length

Lending Club offers loans in two terms, 30 and 60 month terms. Table 9 outlines the effects of a 60-month term loan over. one that is 36 months. Based on the loan's grade, the effect of the 60-month loan could be a 5, or 6-step reduction. Therefore, a loan of 60 months will yield higher interest rates, however, they also come with greater risk.

Tab 9: Risk Modifier for the loan term

Continue with Jack as well as Jill both have requested for a loan for 36 months, meaning their risk modifier is zero, Jack remains a B1 and Jill is a B4.

Step 8 - Find out the final rate

Utilizing Table 10 which is similar to Table 1 at the beginning of this chapter Lending Club would determine that Jack's rate of interest (Grade B1) will be 10.16 percent, and Jill's rate for a loan with a grade B4 would be 13.11%. In spite of the fact that Jill has a higher credit score (725 against. 714) in reality, she's paying a higher rate of interest over Jack because of the amount she's requesting.

This particular example is crucial since, when you examine the notes, there are investors who be wary of loans that aren't A quality, believing that they'll lose their investment. However it isn't always the scenario. Remember our first lesson when we discussed the likelihood that the loan could be in default within 24 months? Someone with a high FICO score is more likely fail but , with Lending Club, it is possible to pay a higher rate of interest than people with a lower credit rating and a greater chance of default.

My opinion is that FICO Score is higher than sub-grade. If I could locate an loan with 700+ FICO Score and is graded either B or C these are the dream loans.

Table 10 Table 10 - Interest Rates

Chapter 3: Establishing Your Loan Criteria

Every lender has an underwriter team who decide what the company's most basic lending requirements should be in relation to the risk level the company is willing to accept and the amount of they would like to receive in compensation in relation to that risk.

Lending Club helps us by setting some fundamental standards for us to adhere to, like not approving loans for someone who has an FICO score less than 660, not approving a person with more than 9 inquiries in the last six months. It is also not possible to approve anyone who has less than 3 years of credit history, and not approving a person with a credit card utilization of more than 98 percent or more.

I would suggest you go further and design your own set of criteria to support your goals for investing.

My objective with any investment is to maximize the return over the return on investment.

To make sure I get my money back, I've set up my own criterion which lets me quickly go through the many available notes and narrow down the ones that fit my lending criteria. One of the advantages offered by Lending Club is that I can set your own filters or criteria, and save them for later use. When I want to revisit notes, I am able to add my filters and view the loan requests that meets my criteria.

The next section we'll look at each of the 26 loan filters that you could pick from. It will be apparent that certain of the filters contain an * at end, which signifies that it is one of the filters I use for my investments. I will explain the reasons behind it and the way I utilize it.

In the beginning first, click Browse Notes (see the letter A in Figure 2.) and then on the left on the right side of the page, you will find the section for filter notes (see the letter B on Figure 2.) and select additional filters. This will bring forth an "add the filter boxes". This is where you'll select the filters you would like to use.

Figure 2 - Notes on Browsing and the addition of filters

Interest Rate*

It's pretty simple It allows you to select what interest rates you would like to look at in my instance, and I would like to look at the entire range. The filter you choose is an option that lets you select any loans, or loans according to their sub-grade (A between A and G). If you were only looking for the loans with "A" graded, then you can select "A" only, and this is all you'd see. In the next chapter the criteria I'm using and the reasons.

Figure 3 Figure 3 - Interest Rate Filter

The purpose of the loan

This filter lets you decide what kind of loans you're willing to finance. Table 11 displays the default rates for each the type of loan. It also lists the default rates of "A" or "B" loan types. Other Loan Purposes, Renewal Energy loans, Small Business loans and Education loans are all close to or much higher than the overall default rate. Therefore, I have excluded them from my list of loans that I would like to put my money into.

Max Loan Amount : Up to

It's an adjustable slider bar that allows you to decide the amount of loan you're willing to take part in and the amount of the loan isn't an issue for me.

Review StatusReview Status

If you select this filter, it will display only loans that have been approved. A part of the approval process requires the borrower to supply important documents such as the payroll details as well as other documents. If you don't choose "Approved" as an option, there's possibility that the borrower's application won't be accepted or they will fail to supply the necessary documents which could cause the loan to not being approved. In this case, you could have wasted your wait for the loan's be credited however, you could have seen the money in your account sooner.

I am only interested in reviewing loans which have been approved. it indicates that the person who is borrowing is determined to complete the loan and is working hard to see the loan completed.

Verified Income

Lending Club does not verify the income of every single applicant, according to my experience, less than 10% of loans contain this information. If you look through this option, you'll only see a tiny fraction of loans that are available.

Funding Progress

This allows you to focus on loans that have already funded to a certain percentage. Lending Club will not approve any loan that doesn't attain a 60% financing amount before the time for review expires. If you only want to view loans that have reached an amount of funding This filter allows you to narrow down the loans.

The listing expires on

This filter lets you to narrow the loan down to the amount of time that is left prior to the time the offer expires. you have the option of all, seven days or less, or 3 days, or less.

Exclude Relisted Loans

This filter allows you to eliminate loans that were not funded in the past.

*CREDIT Score

This filter lets you to select which credit scores you're ready to take on. The options include Any 6, 660-678. 679-713. 714-749, 750-779 or 780+.

My personal preference is to select all but the 660-678 as their default rates for this group is 4.40 percent..

Table 12 shows the default rate based on credit score.

Max Ratio Debt-to-Income

The ratio of a person's debt-to-income is the sum of monthly debt payments multiplied into their annual income. By using this filter, you'll be able select the highest ratio of debt-to-income that your borrowers must be able to attain in order to meet the investment requirements.

I'm seeking the borrowers who have a debt-to-income ratio between 15 and 34%. I'll explain why during the subsequent chapter.

The earliest credit line

This filter lets you decide the length of record of credit the borrower holds. The options are any length of credit one years or longer, five years, or more and 10 years or more.

Max Open Credit Lines

This filter lets you limit the number of open credit lines a borrower is allowed to open. you have the option of choosing any, 10 maximum 20, 20 maximum, or 30 maximum.

Total Credit Lines

Similar to Max Open Credit lines, this filter lets you sort loans according to the total amount of credit lines. The options are similar to Max Open Credit Lines.

Revolving Credit Balance

This filter lets you define the maximum revolving balance you wish the borrower to hold. A Revolving credit balance is the sum amount of the balances in all credit accounts. You have the option of any, less than $100,000, less than $50,000 or less than $15,000. If you're concerned that a person who is borrowing might have excessive credit, this filter can help to lessen the risk.

Revolving Balance Utilization

This filter lets you limit the amount of credit balance revolving you would like the borrower to enjoy. This is the proportion of the borrower's amount to the credit limit. For instance when a person's total credit card balances revolving of $5,000, and their credit card limit totals are $10,000, the revolving balance utilization will be 50%..

Inquiries over the last 6 months*

This filter lets you filter out people who are seeking loans or credit cards. I prefer only to look at loans when the borrower has had less than three inquiries in the past 6 months.

Months since the last delinquency

This filter lets you specify the minimum length of time that the borrower has been in arrears on a loan. The minimum I have set is 36 month.

Home Ownership

This filter lets you select a specific borrower on their residence ownership. you can select from your own rent, mortgage, or none.

The minimum length of employment

This filter lets you to specify the minimum amount of time you wish the borrower to work for at their current position.

One working for a period of 10or more years has an average default percentage of 2.97 percent, while those who have worked for less than one year has an default of 4.25 percent.

Location State

The state's economy will affect the ability of its citizens to pay back their loans. In the moment, the default rate of Lending Club is 3.33% To show how the default rates of loans is affected by economic conditions, look at these two instances.

The unemployment rate currently of Florida is 8.5 percent, and the default rates of Lending Club loans from Florida is 4.74 percent. Compare that with states like Oklahoma where the unemployment rate currently stands at 5.3 percent and the default rate for loans is 2.73 percent. This filter will allow you to remove states with an even higher default rate.

You can find the unemployment rates currently in each state by visiting this site:

http://www.bls.gov/web/laus/laumstrk.htm

Public RecordsPublic Records

This filter lets you block borrowers who have public information on their credit reports. Public records include judgmentsand foreclosures, lawsuits and wage attachments, bankruptcy filings, federal and state tax lien as well as past-due child support. The information is reported by state, county, as well as federal court to various credit reporting agencies.

I exclude borrowers with publicly available documents from my search for loans.

Delinquencies (Last 2 yrs.)

This filter lets you remove loans when the borrower has suffered an amount of delinquencies in the past two years. My ideal candidate for borrowing is one who has not experienced an outstanding delinquency during the past three years.

Exclude loans that have already been invested in*

This filter lets you not review loans that you've already made an investment in. This is a method to make sure that you don't make a second investment with the same loan that you made an investment in another time.

I've chosen this option to ensure that I do not invest more in loans than I'm confident about.

Terms (36 - 60 months)

This filter allows you to view loans with either a 36 month term or a 60-month period.

This is a matter of individual preference. If you're looking to increase the yield, then include 60-month loan in the portfolio. in the event that you want to reduce risk, I would recommend limiting the amount of 60-month loans you own. By focusing on only 36-month loans, you lower your default risk by 17 basis points (2.04 percent (1.87% - 1.87 percent = .17 percent) however, the interest rate you earn is reduced by at 115 basis point (12.85 percent (11.70%) - 11.70 percent = 1.15 percent) I believe you're sacrificing an amount of money for just a slight increase in the default rate.

Chapter 4: My Credit Criteria

In the previous chapter, I explained the ways to filter loans so that you can set your own lending criteria. I highlighted with asterisks those filters I employ in making investment decision.

In this chapter, I'm going to go through my most popular filters and explain how each affects the rates of default and interest rate. To complete this, I'm going to use the P2P back testing site, NickelStreamRoller.com.

NickelStreamRoller.com is an awesome site that collects all of the data from both Lending Club and Prosper.com and it allows you to see the impact that your filters will have on your yield and your default rate.

In this chapter, when I speak of an interest rate it is the amount the borrower pays, it is not inclusive of any defaults, or even fees like the Lending Club 1% loan management fee.

To establish the standard, as of this moment the default interest rate stands at 3.33 percent and the average rate of interest is 12.55 percent. These figures will be used as a reference. As I construct my model, using filters, I aim to reduce the default rate and still maintain an interest rate. When we look through these figures, I will discuss more.

Interest Rate

In this section, I've chosen the loan grades B, A B and E. You're probably wondering why there's no C or D. It's common sense to say that loans graded E have higher risk and carry more of a chance of default than loans that have C or D ratings. However, according to my analysis of Lending Club stats, that's not the situation. The figure 4 illustrates that the the default rate for E Graded Loans is 4.999 percent, while C as well as D rates of default are 6.296 percent and 8.073 percentages, respectively. In this section, you'll see the outcomes of excluding C's and D's.

Figure 4 Data for Grade

Lending Purpose

As I have shown in Table 11 which I also included below The purpose of the loan has an effect upon the percentage of default. Due to this correlation I have decided not to make loan to Medical, Other, Renewal Energy, Small Business and Education.

After eliminating these four loan objectives The default rate increases to 2.9 percent, while the interest rate rises to 12.57 percent. Thus, both numbers improve as because of eliminating those reasons for loans that don't work effectively.

Table 11-Default Rate according to the purpose of the loan

Score on Credit

In this instance I will eliminate loans that have credit scores below 679. This increases the default percentage to 2.63 percent and lowers the cost of borrowing to 11.6 percent. People with poor credit score are charged a higher interest and, by using the filter I'm removing those people off the table which is why my interest rate decreases .95 percent which is 95 basis point.

Max Ratio of Debt to Income

A preferred lender has a ratio of debt to income ratio that is between 15% to 35%. When you apply this filter the default rate rises only a little bit to 2.6 percent and the rate increases to the rate of interest to 12.07 percent.

Inquiries over the last six months

My most preferred lender has 0-3 inquiries within the last six months, and more than three then the default interest rate is increased between 0 and 3. the default rate rises to 2.42 percent while the rate of interest increases to 12.05 percent.

Months Since the Last Delinquency

Three years of timely payment is my normal for me, so I set the limit to 36 month. This reduces default rates to 2.39 percent, and increases it to 12.87 percent.

Public Records

As you are aware I like to avoid the borrowers who have public information on their credit reports and this reduces the default percentage to 2.04 per cent and reduces my interest rate to 12.85 percent.

In the case of borrowers who have public documents is 8.11 percent..

Keep your Filters

Once you've established your loan requirements You can save your filters so that when you come back to look through notes, you can use the filters, as well. Lending Club will automatically filter out loans that don't match your requirements.

It's also helpful when you set different criteria for different types of loans. For instance, if, for example, you'd like to be more cautious about Medical Loans, you can add that to the filters. Lending Club will always show you what loans you could consider.

Connecting it all

When you plug these filters into the NickelStreamRoller.com site, you will see that my average default rate is 2.767% and my average yield is 10.929%. Do you recall the place we began? In the beginning, we had a default of 3.33 percent, with an interest average of 12.55 percent. The filters cut my default rates by 56 basis point (.56 percent) and also reduced my rates by 161 basis point (1.61%).).

Chapter 5: Making An Investment

After you've created your lending criteria , you are now ready to begin your investment.

When you click the "invest" button (see the letter C on Figure 5), Lending Club will take you to the location in which you will be able to access those saved filters (see the letter D in Figure 5).).

Choose the filters you want to open.

If you click on the name of the filter, Lending Club will now only display notes that match the criteria for your investment. In the figure 6, you can see that Lending Club has filtered 751 down to 11 to review.

Figure 5 Application of Filters

Figure 6 Application of Filters

The section that says, "Build a Portfolio from ..." (see Figure 6) opens up more information about the notes that satisfy the requirements.

The second step will be to arrange the columns by interest rate. to do this, simply click on the column header with the word "Rate".

Figure 7 lists the available loans that meet my needs. The loans I'm the most interested are ones that have the highest rate of interest and the highest rating, so in this instance I'm looking at notes with ratings of B3 and A5. There is a note that's rated D1 and paying 17.77 percent. I'll explain how to invest in a note such as this in Chapter 7, but for we'll just say that it this doesn't meet my buy-and-hold investment strategy.

Figure 7 - Notes Available

Pulling the Trigger

If you're satisfied with the loan you have chosen and are looking to invest You simply have to select the box in the column called "Investment" and then enter the amount you would like to invest, and then click"Add" or "Add Button" that appears in the lower left corner of the box. Before you can do that it is necessary to decide the amount you wish to invest.

I strongly believe in maintaining a diverse portfolio. If you have $5,000 in loan funds You could put that money in one note, or $25 for 200 notes. I would prefer taking 200 note. Even if the capital of your portfolio was greater, I would opt for smaller investments and greater loans. In a research conducted by Lending Club, they looked at the size of portfolios of investors. They discovered that when investors had more than 800 notes, the investor earned a positive return. 93% of the investors saw returns between 6 and 18 percent.

My suggestion is to begin with $25 loans , until you have about 800 note in the portfolio ($20,000 worth of account) Then, you can increase your loan amount.

After you have selected the investments you want to invest in and have you have entered the amount of your investment then click"Add To Order. "Add to Purchase" button, and follow the steps to finish your investment.

The balance you have available will be reduced by the amount you've invested in these loans, despite the fact that the loan will not be repaid immediately.

After the note has been fully funded or the advertising period is over The note will then be delivered to the Lending Club closers to actually finish the loan. They collaborate with the borrower to get the loan documentation approved and to set up the repayment procedure. This is usually just a matter of time and Lending Club will advise you via email when the loan is funded.

There are instances that a loan doesn't get funded or be funded. This could be the result of the inability to fund from other investors, or when the borrower's decision not to take on the loan, or there are other reasons which prevent the loan from taking place. If this occurs you'll receive an email from them advising that the loan didn't pay off as well as that funds were transferred to the account you have and available to invest.

Chapter 6: Following The Investment

The difficult part is over and the investment has been made the loan to a stranger and in this chapter we will examine what happens following the loan funds.

From my experience, there are five results:

1.) The lender pays back the loan during the term of loan.

2.) The borrower chooses to repay the loan in advance.

3.) The borrower chooses to not pay for the loan.

4.) You are required to be taxed on the interest and profits made.

5.) Then you choose to sell your loan to make profits

Let's take a look at the various occasions.

Paying in Time

In this scenario, if the borrower makes their payment on time each and every month your account will get credit with the portion of the monthly installment and you'll see your balance rise. As the cash balance grows, you will continue the processof following your method and investing time, increasing your balance. You'll always be grateful you bought this book and you've concluded it to be the best investment you could have made.

The borrower pays for the loan early.

Certain investors see this as a positive thing some see this as a good thing, while others view it as a problem. Let's examine both aspects. The first thought that comes to mind when you think the reason for this is that your cash balance is greater than you anticipated. When you examine the details of the loan You will see that the section with fully paid indicates that the loan is paid.

You're probably like me and then you're content to have your money back , and then you go to make another investment. Many investors are disappointed when this happens, particularly in the case of one with a high rate of interest as it is now necessary to reinvest money and there's an opportunity that the money won't be capable of being reinvested at the same rate. This is referred to as the risk of reinvestment.

As there's nothing you can do about it then you'll have to go out and look for a note that you can make an investment in.

The Borrower is now a Deadbeat

As you can see by the moment, my main objective is to return principal. I do not like losing money, therefore, when loans go downwards, which they do be, it is a huge disappointment for me. I've been extremely fortunate in that I have only a handful of loans fail me, and they have given me a good method to limit my risk quickly.

When a borrower is late with the payment, Lending Club is on the case and will contact the borrower. It's great that you won't have to take care of any problems with collection, though, there are times when you want to.

In the majority of cases, Lending Club works to get the borrower to sign the repayment plan, and sometimes this is successful. Sometimes people will be to a payment plan but later not pay In these instances, Lending Club will engage a firm that collects to recover the debt. If this occurs the money can be returned back to you account. As I've seen, this hasn't happened however the debts were eliminated as bad credit.

The Lending Club notes are reported on the credit reports of the borrower and the write-offs be on file for 7 years, further damaging the score of the borrower's credit. Once a loan has been taken out of the system, there's nothing that can be accomplished.

The lessons I've gained from these experiences which is why I monitor the loans with a keen eye and, when a loan is in the grace-time period I place the loan to auction via the exchange platform, at par which is the sum of principal that remains outstanding. I will go over this in the next chapter.

Figure 8 illustrates the loan that was charged Off as not collectable. Prior to the charge off, I recouped $1.22 Interest and Principal on a loan of $25. The principal remaining was $24.47. Following the charge off, I was able to receive an additional $1.07 and the net gain was $22.71.

Figure 8 Charged-off loan

Paying the Taxman

If you do not invest via an IRA or IRA, you'll be liable for tax on interest that you earn as well as the profits you earn through the sale of loans via trade platforms (covered in the following chapter).

If you're investing in small investments, you won't get a 1099-INT, but you are still tax-paying even when the income isn't declared.

Why aren't you able to get 1099-INT? might ask?

The tax code is designed to require Lending Club to issue you an IRS Form 1099-INT in the event that the interest on the loan is more than $10.00. Since loans are not likely to yield enough interest each year, the earnings will not be reported.

In the event that you don't have the tax form until the close of the fiscal year, you'll have access your account and check the end of year statements to figure out how much interest you earned.

It is also necessary to record the profits or loss you make from loans. This is calculated on the profits you earn using the trading platform the sale of your notes , and then , you'll also subtract any debt that is not a good one from the total. This is the net investment income.

Making money from selling loans

This is among my most favorite things that involves loans. If you are doing it correctly, you could make your profit greater than the interest you pay for the loan. In the next article, we'll explore the realm of trading loans.

Chapter 7: Making Profits Out Of The Trading Account

Is it possible to get a better yield than the interest rate of the loan?

Yes , thanks for the platform that allows trading.

In this chapter, I'm going demonstrate how you can profit from loans that are good and minimize your losses when you see that a loan may be headed south.

What is the trading Account?

Trading Account Trading Account is a secondary market that Lending Club has set up to assist investors in managing the risk of liquidity. Without this market, it is nearly impossible to liquidate your assets until the loan was completely paid. Because of your trading account you are able to trade your loans at an income, breakeven or sell them all at once when you are able to price them appropriately.

The Profit Opportunity

It is not possible for everyone to invest directly into loans through the Lending Club platform; some states restrict their residents to make loans investments on an intermediary market also known as The Trading Account as well as trading platform. Trading Platform.

At the time of writing individuals can now make loans investments if they reside in: California, Colorado, Connecticut, Delaware, Florida, Georgia, Hawaii, Idaho, Illinois, Kentucky, Louisiana, Maine, Minnesota, Missouri, Mississippi, Montana, New Hampshire, Nevada, New York, Rhode Island, South Carolina, South Dakota, Utah, Virginia, Washington, Wisconsin, West Virginia and Wyoming. If you reside in a state that is not listed in this article, continue reading this chapter as I will demonstrate how to apply the strategies that are discussed in this chapter even if you need to purchase the loan initially on an auction.

To demonstrate the possibility to illustrate the opportunity, imagine Rob who is an investor comes from Michigan decides to sign up for the Lending Club account, because Rob wants to earn 8%+ return on his investment. However, when he signs up, the account he discovers that he cannot lend directly due to Michigan law. The only way to fund his loan is to sign up for a trading account and then invest in the secondary market. That is where the chance to earn profit is.

Seasoned or Not

An investment that's experienced is one with an outstanding payment history. According to my experience, most of the buyers who use this platform want experienced loans. However, I haven't had success selling loans that are not seasoned through using the account for trading. My success was achieved after the note had two payment.

Yield to Call

Before we dive into this topic we must first discuss some basic bond math, and more specifically Yield To Call. Do not worry, I'll simplify this.

Yield to Call is a calculation to determine the yield on any cash flow (loan or bond) that is held until the call date or in our case a sales datwww.thebookonp2plending.come. It's an equation that allows you to know the true yield depending on the amount of cash you get.

If you're curious about learning more about the formula, the guru is Dr. Google (google.com), will be happy to take you to numerous websites that will show you precisely the method to determine this figure. To make it easy for you, I've made an excel spreadsheet which allows users to input some details and, boom it will calculate your return. It is possible to access the excel spreadsheet on the books site: http://ytcfile.com.

How to Sell Your Product at Profit

The first step is to select the right note. In the case of this note, I purchased the D1-note in the month of July 2012 with an interest rate of 17.27 percent.

Figure 9 - One of my loans

When I took out the loan, I bought it with the intention of sell it within some time; my objective was to increase the yield above the initial interest rate for the loan. To achieve this, you must first to make an investment in an interest-rate loan that is high this means that I must give up my FICO score of minimum. For this loan, my initial FICO score of 670-674. I decided to try my luck on it since it met all my other criteria. After I purchase an account with the intention to sell, I let the loan to mature for 2 to four months in the hopes that they'll pay their bills punctually and that the credit rating will increase.

Figure 10 illustrates the performance of the loan for this loan. You can observe that the borrower completed 4 payments in time, in addition to their credit scores having increased.

Figure 10 - Performance of Loan Page

Figure 11 illustrates that you can see how the FICO Score has improved. it's now in the 724-720 range.

Figure 11 - Change in Credit Score

Thus, the borrower has stayed to the terms of the bargain. They are using the loan money in order to settle their debts They are making their payments as well as their credit rating has improved due to this and this is an ideal loan to offer for sale at profits.

The Price Setting

In this article I will explain how to determine an exact value for a note in markets that are secondary. It is possible to use this method of valuing a note when you're buying or selling. To accomplish this, we're going to need to revisit the 8 steps in Chapter 2. To demonstrate how this process works. I've outlined these steps.

Step 1. the borrower's FICO(r) Score

A borrower's FICO(r) score is currently 724 - 720; Table 2 indicates that the loan is within the sub-grade of A5. To be precise, FICO will place them in the A4 or the A5 range I prefer the more conservative option.

Step 2: What is the borrower asking for?

The borrower asked for $18,000. Table 3 states that their maximum loan amount is $15,000, thus they're requesting 120 percent of the guidelines and this lowers the subgrade of 4 (Table 4) and they are now on B4 ratings.

Step 3 - The number of credit inquiries

The loan application from the beginning shows that they did not have any inquiries in the last six months. Table 5 states they receive an additional modifier of +1, which puts them into sub-group B3.

Step 4 - Length of Credit in Months

The first credit line date in April 2003, which is 113 months. Table 6 states that they remain within the same sub-group B3.

Step 5 - The number of open Accounts

The original application lists 15 open accounts. Table 7 indicates that there is no changes in their sub-groups, remaining at B3.

Step 6 - Revolving Credit Utilization

The initial application indicates that the credit utilization as 79%. Table 8 shows no changes in the sub-group B3.

Step 7 - Step 7 -

36-months, Table 9 states there is no change in sub-groups, but still B3.

Step 8 - Find out the final rate

Table 10 shows the interest rate for a B3 loan is 12.12 percent. If the loan was made today it could be an 12.12 per cent interest loan, compared to the 17.27 percent that the current rate.

To calculate the present value (Present Value) of this loan, we're using an online Financial calculator for calculating the current value. I'll walk by the process. If you're interested in using one, I'm currently using an iPhone application called 12E calc which is an emulator of HP 12E, which is an HP 12E financial calculator and it's great.

The first step is to note the remaining payments The loan was a 36-month one and there were four installments, and there are 32 that remain. Enter 32 and press"N".

Figure 12 - Total number of payments

The rate of interest is now 12.12 percent, so enter 12.12 and press the g button , and then press the i button. This transforms the annual interest rate to a monthly rate (1.01).

Figure 13: Converting interest to monthly

Figure 14 Inputing the Monthly Interest Rate

The next one is the current month's payment of $.89 You enter .89 and then press to activate the PMT (Payment) key.

Figure 15 : Current Pay Amount

Once the loan has been fully paid, the value in the future will be zero, so type in zero and press on the key FV.

The Future Value is set to zero

You must now find the Present Value. To solve this problem, you need to press on the key PV.

Figur 17-Calculating the Value of the Present

The screen now informs that the present value of this loan is $24.23 in comparison to. an outstanding principal of $22.83 This means that you can offer the loan through the platform for trading and then sell it at an $1.40 gain.

Figure 18 What is the present value (Current Value)

Side Note

The actual display shows -24.23 which means that it's an outflow of cash. That is, the buyer is paying for -24.23.

To calculate the yield of the loan if it was sold at $24.23 we could turn to Excel's Excel yield-to-call spreadsheet. The results indicate that the yield from the transaction would be 33.56 percent.

Figure 19 - Yield Calculation

This is how you manually appraise a note. However, there are two caveats when pricing a note in this manner first, it's quite time-consuming it could take anywhere from 5 to 10 minutes to gather all the data, examine the tables. Then, put the data into the calculator. In this next article, I'll demonstrate the method I use to price them quickly. As with everything else supply and demand determines the price. Buyers in the secondary market might not take the time to calculate the appropriate price It's an important thing to understand, however, I'm convinced there's an easier way.

Pricing The Quick Way

If I'm selling the note via the trading platform, that has the borrower's great credit history and the borrower's credit score has improved, I try selling the note at between 3% and 4% of the principal outstanding as well as accrued interest. Even after I calculated manually the note's value in the previous section the markup of the sale price to the principle and the accrued amount of interest is 5.15 percent. If I could quickly place the note up for sale with an 3.5 percentage or 4.0 percent markup, I could leave some cash and yield on the table, but I'd be able to save myself some effort, and remember that it's time to make money. Additionally even if I have put it on the market at a reasonable price, does not necessarily mean that someone will purchase it. They are also looking to increase their return.

In the remainder of this section, I'll walk you through the process of pricing your note with the flat rate mark-up. In the beginning, you'll have to be aware of the important fundamental.

Figure 19 shows the principal outstanding and accrued interest of Lending Club's "My Notes" section of Lending Club.

The Figure 19 is a Section taken from my Note

In this case , the outstanding principal in this case is $22.83 while the Accrued Incentive (interest due to me, but I haven't yet collected) will be $.21.

Utilizing this file, the Yield To Call Calculation Excel file, you'll need to enter the following data:

The face value (Investment) for the loan: $25.00

"The Outstanding Principal," $22.83

Its Accrued Incentives: $.21

The interest rate of the loan: 17.27 percent

The amount of time the loan was held 4

A Markup, or Mark Down I desire: 3.3%

Once you have entered this information after which you can be able to see the sales price of the loan as well as yield to call or in another manner the yield you will earn if you sell your home now.

Table 20 Yield at a 3 % Markup

In the end, by selling the loan in just a few monthsI'm in a position increase my income from 17.27 percent to 27.44 percent annually.

The increase in yield isn't for without cost. The reason you're increasing your yield and earning profit is that the buyer's yield is 13.75 percent that is less than the amount of your loan. If you've ever made an investment in bonds and bonds, it's similar to selling the bond at a higher price.

Then why would your client prefer an interest rate that is lower than the rate of interest? It's simple - because the credit score of the borrower has improved, they're assuming that they will be able to take on a less risk than the one you took and, as a result, they are more willing to take the lower interest rate. You've taken a significant amount of the risk off the loan.

When you evaluate the manual pricing process for an investment as we did initially, to the present value to simply picking the desired price, you'll be able to see that the difference in profit is around $.50 or six12 basis point (6.12 percent). In the end, the buyer decides the price of the note. If they feel it's too expensive or too low, it will not be sold.

3 Things to Take into Consideration

There are three points to consider when putting an offer for a loan in the account of trading.

The first is that the amount of interest accrued on the loan is increasing every day. This is crucial, as the loan is available for trade on your trading account a maximum of one week. During this time, the accrued interest will continue rise, and should you not be able to figure out the amount of accrued interest to be over the next seven days, you could be settling for a lower interest rate.

To calculate the daily increment of interest accrued, you need to calculate the principal outstanding ($22.83) and divide this by interest rates (.1727 or 17.27 percent) and that will give you the annual amount of interest earned of which you will get $3.94. Divide that number by the number of 365 (days in the year) for a total amount of $.0108. That means that from the moment you start to the date of next loan payment the interest that accrued will increase by $.0108 every day. As you prepare to put the note on sale I suggest adding seven days from accrued interests (to the sales price) which is in this instance, an additional $.075 (8 cents) to the $.21 current value).

If you were fortunate enough to be able to sell the note on the first dayof trading, it would yield 28.42 percent.

The other reason to be aware of is the fact that there is a charge to sell your trades on the Trading Account It's 1percent, so when you sell an investment for $23.73 the amount you pay is $.24. If you're using the Excel spreadsheet for calculating the return, that charge is already factored into the return, therefore what you see is the result of the cost of 1.

The third factor to consider is that, like all things that is offered for sale, the economics are in play. If buyers feel that your price is too expensive the buyer may decide not to purchase it. There aren't any alternatives in this and in the event that the note isn't sold consider the price and adjust the price accordingly.

What happens if there's any improvement of credit

What happens to those notes in which the credit score didn't increase or get worse? When the rate of interest is extremely high I will still put them on the market at between 2% and 3.3% markup. This is because there are many states that allow residents to invest directly, and you're serving as an intermediary for the residents. Yes, you are able to sell these notes and earn profits.

What is the minimum time I will need to keep the loan?

There is no need to wait for 4 months to attempt to sell a note. I usually sell them shortly after the first installment, it might take a bit of time to make it sell, but I will continue listing them for auction. It is free to put the loan as a sale item but only if it sells.

My loan didn't sell

It's fine, but you must examine your calculations, alter the price as needed and then list it again.

The loan is headed south

As you are aware I've experienced a couple of loans which defaulted on me. This obviously doesn't meet my objective of having my entire principal returned. Therefore, when I notice an account that is entering its grace time, I immediately take action and offer it for auction through this trading site. I typically put this loan up for sale at a one percent markup of my principal balance plus accrued interests. If it does not sell at this rate I'll lower it to the value of my principal balance and continue the reduction to 1percent until it is sold. If it is able to return to its condition that is current, I then put the loan on the market for the one percent markup. My aim is to get the credit off my records and allow someone else to get it.

This loan method lets me cut my losses rapidly and retain my capital.

Do they buy loans during this grace time? Absolutely. How many people were purchasing Enron stock when they were headed toward zero? Many.

When I was rereading the chapter I found an entry in the grace period. I posted it on the market but it didn't go through. The listing time was during which the account was updated and I then relisted it at 1% of the price and it sold within a single day. I don't want to hold onto an account where the lender is in financial trouble. It's more beneficial to dispose of it at a bargain rather than letting the loan fall into default. Learn to cut losses before they become too big and you'll be able to get a higher overall profit.

Chapter 8: Buy And Sell On The Trading Platform

You might be in one of the states where you aren't able to direct invest in loans, or you'd like to look into a different method of investment in loans In this instance, as you go through the notes offered for sale through the Trading Platform You will notice that the filters don't exist, and the user interface isn't easy to navigate So let me demonstrate how I discover the loans that enable you to make money and increase your balance.

Then, when you are logged into the Trading Platform then click on Browse Notes (see figure 21).

Diagram 21 Notes for Trading Platform

Figure 22 illustrates how I instantly change the settings of the page:

Status Never Late, remove all other options as I would not like to buy notes that are late.

The remaining payments: I alter this number to 35. I'd like to confirm that at the very least one payment has been paid.

Figure 22 - The Platform Settings I use

Then , I hit then the Search button. This should eliminate loans that I am not interested in. Once the page is refreshed I then hit the last column, "Yield to Maturity" two times to sort it from the highest to the lowest.

Then I search to get the highest yield when my credit score is increasing. In my search to write this article I received a variety of loans that met the requirements, but they require a bit of review to decide if I would like to invest in these loans.

Figure 23 Notifications about the Trading Platform

When you look into a specific loan's performance, you'll be able to see in the upper right-hand corner, a link that will bring you back to the loan's original listing to examine what the original investor was seeing prior to making the investment on the loan. The good thing is that you can see what that they did not know, such as a history of payments and evidence that your credit score is increasing.

It is evident, there are numerous loans listed on this page which have an acceptable Yield to maturity to permit me to purchase and list the loan again as described in the final chapter. This allows anyone to make a bet on the loans and then list them through the trading platform for profit-making sales. Selling a note for an increase after just one or two days of holding it drives the yield will be sky-high. All you need to do is wash and repeat.

Chapter 9: What Is Peer-To Peer Lending?

In the past when a person required a loans for the purchase of a home or car then he would have visit an institution like a bank or financial institution to obtain the loan. The applicant had to submit an application for the loan, and wait for it to be granted. Banks typically approve and deny loans on the basis of the credit score of the borrower. A person's credit score was generally assessed based on the amount they earned and what their financial status was.

However, today the situation is different. It is now easier to obtain money or even loans. Websites, like Lending Club, for instance Lending Club, have started to compete with banks and financial institutions by permitting real-time interaction with people. In the present, if a person is in need of borrowing money the person does not have to visit the bank. It is possible to use peer-to peer lending and take money from someone else.

What is Peer-to-Peer (P2P) Loans?

Peer-to peer (P2P) loan is a different option to the traditional bank-intermediated lending. The lenders and the borrowers communicate with one another on an online platform. In recent years, P2P lending has grown in popularity. Apart from Lending Club, other P2P sites, like Society One, Balmain Private and Ratesetter have also come on board.

Peer-to-peer lending refers to crowdsourcing loans. It's about persuading other people to support you in coming up with an idea. For instance, KickStarter is a website to crowd-fund. It lets users fund their projects.

Loans are available to those who want to borrow that are backed by private investors, not financial institutions and banks. Of course, like every other loan the loans are accompanied by the same rates of interest. When they apply for a loan, they submit their forms to the website, exactly as they would the bank. The team of the platform then starts checking their application information (such as like their identity as well as their employment status and their credit score). They also evaluate the risk associated with the loan and decide on the interest rates applicable prior to posting the application on their site.

Lendersthen go through the applications and select applicants they wish to assist. They may help in a limited or full way. Once the load is fully funded, the platform will transfer the money in the loan to the creditor. The users of these platforms are also required to pay an amount.

After the loan is completed after the loan is completed, the website platform takes over loan service. They will be responsible for making repayments and managing late payments. If the borrower fails to pay the platform handles to collect the debt, and the lender is responsible for the loss.

Peer-to-peer lending is extremely popular with investors since it allows them to loan tiny amounts to borrowers, and earn interest on a continuous basis as borrower pays back their loans. The majority of P2P loans serve to settle debts with a lower interest. If you're trying to pay off credit card debt then you should consider P2P lending.

What is the purpose in Peer-toPeer (P2P) lending?

P2P lending grows rapidly due to the fact that it fills gaps in the credit market. In general there are two main reasons for why P2P lending is a reality.

In the beginning, it is unsecured personal loans that banking institutions and banks have a hard time to get at competitive rates. These loans are designed to be used for smaller amounts, but have a the burden of having to construct and maintain.

In general, the banks as well as financial establishments would prefer to provide credit cards to the borrowers as they offer higher rates of interest as well as ongoing revenue from transactions and perpetual loan terms.

P2P lending is characterized by less cost contrasted to traditional banks. Therefore, P2P lending websites offer significantly lower interest rates. These are the factors that draw potential borrowers to sign up for a loan.

Furthermore, P2P lending provides the prospect of a huge return for the investor. A net return of 6% - 25% is highly appealing and is much better than a bank deposit rate.

When Did Peer-toPeer (P2P) Beginning of Lending Begin?

Peer-to peer lending has been in use since 2005. It has been in existence for a total of eleven years. Its origins are in capital markets. Over the course of thousands of years the capital market and the borrowers were brought together through non-bank lenders. For many years, corporate ownership has been splintered through stock exchanges.

Peer-to peer lending is an industry which is growing rapidly. For instance, take Lending Club and Prosper, for example. They've seen 147% growth in just 12 months. This proves that peer-to peer lending is becoming more well-known with every day. It definitely offers a number of advantages for borrowers as well as investors as well.

Borrowers

Since 2008, the banks as well as other financial institutions were hit by massive financial losses. Actually they continue to suffer the consequences to this day. Many people who had no difficulty to apply by banks and other financial organizations in previous years, suddenly were faced with financial difficulties. Many people have turned to their homes equity portfolios to secure loans over the last decade. But, as houses across in the United States dropped in value as the economy weakened, financial institutions and banks were more cautious in the approval of loans. They stopped providing unsecured personal loans. This led to lots of people resorted to credit cards that are much easier to obtain. However, these credit cards also came with more expensive rates of interest.

Then, peer to peer lending came into the picture and was able to fill the gap in the market for consumer finance. The people were finally able to free themselves from interest charges on credit cards. Peer-to-peer lending means that the credit card's 28% interest rate could be cut by half. That is an enormous relief for those who are borrowers. The fixed loan term , which generally lasts between three and five years, is appealing to the borrowers as they can calculate how long they'll be able to pay their obligations. They can also determine the ways to repay the debt completely within the shortest amount of time.

Different types of Borrowers

In general there are three primary kinds of borrowers: property-based consumer, company, and property-based. It is possible to invest in these types of loans. be an ideal option for investors.

Investors

It's not just the borrower people who find peer-to-peer lending attractive. Investors also believed it could be profitable. They were enthralled by the notion that it could provide the highest rates of return.

Indeed, some investors have earned minimum 10% of their annual earnings. They have more than 6%..

Investors have the option of deciding on the degree of risk they are willing to take when it comes to peer-to-peer lending. Investors can invest in loans of the grade A with excellent credit ratings and the risk of default are very low. You can also choose to invest in loans that have higher interest rates and greater risk. Better yet, they could decide to combine of high risk and low risk loans.

Many investors are happy that they invest in real people and not just a banks or mutual funds. The funds are invested in credit for consumers, and this is distinct from the other types of investment options. They also have the ability to provide diversification to their portfolios by utilizing peer-to-peer lending.

How risky or secure is Peer-to-Peer (P2P) lending?

Peer-to-peer lending can vary from good to bad. The United States, subprime lending has shown that P2P lending improperly handled, could result in more than 50 percent in default rate. In contrast the majority of loans to borrowers with good credit score get an average of default rates less than 1percent.

The primary test for P2P lending is likely to occur when a new economic downturn takes place. Many P2P borrowers live in a modest lifestyle between pay check through pay cheque. If they did have savings whatsoever it's not likely to be the case that they take out loans. Also, they probably don't own any significant assets to sell.

As unemployment increases the higher the likelihood that default rates for P2P loans will also be more likely to rise. The available data for prior financial crises aren't as extensive, however.

P2P lending is gaining popularity in the United States is not the only country where P2P lending is gaining popularity. Within the United Kingdom, P2P lending is also one of the fastest-growing markets. Customers are increasingly turning to online platforms due to their attractive interest rates.

However, even if the results look appealing but can you really say they're enough for high-risk type of lending? So, removing banks and establishing an equitable financial network that connects borrower with lenders, in a cost-effective setting is an excellent idea.

However, there's an issue; this is because the more the industry grows more risky. In a typical credit situation, a higher risk equals high returns. In this particular type of environment the demands of investors who want to earn high returns are driving down rates from other types of assets.

The current economic conditions are a risk. Risks are often misvalued. It's very simple to lend money, however returning it can be a bit difficult. Plus, this may also be a challenge during recessions.

A solid Track Records and Safety Funds

The dangers are evident. However, the track record is extremely positive. For example, Zopa, which is the largest lender in the nation has a 10-year track record of achieving returns. Investors can be at ease knowing that they can enjoy excellent returns.

As per Giles Andrews, Zopa's chief executive, the experiences of the company in the financial crisis has shaped the business exists today. In reality, Zopa has managed to endure the credit crisis without capital losses to investors and only some returns losses in the year 2008.

As with many P2P lending sites, Zopa also offers a amount of protection against reserve funds. In reality, it has created its own Zopa Safeguard Trust, which is able to pay for any losses that could occur. The trust was launched in 2013 and currently covers PS344m out of PS500m remaining loans.

Zopa's trust for safeguards accounts for 1.9pc from their loans, while their most severe percentage of defaults was 5.54 percent in 2008. Yet, Andrews claimed that their investors have not suffered any net loss, even during the 2008 financial crisis.

Another popular P2p lending business, Ratesetter, also has an impressive track record. It was founded in the year 2010, and this is the reason it doesn't have a figures for the year the year 2008. However, the rate of default on loans has been below 2 percent which is believed as safe. The company has surpassed its expectations in the past; however, it was just once and that was in the first year of its existence. In the years since, however, the business has always returned the money of its investors.

Chapter 10: Becoming A Peer-To-Peer Lender

For the majority of P2P loan platforms signing up process is easy and fast. You will need to supply vital personal details as you normally would. Then, you need to follow the registration procedure. Once you've done that, you will be able to figure out how much you're willing to lend the borrower and for the length of time. It is also necessary to transfer the funds to your account online. As an investor, you're in the control of your money. This means that you can start making loans immediately if you wish.

The requirements for becoming an investor

In many P2P loan platforms companies and individuals can also become investors as long as they satisfy the standards for the process.

To begin, prospective investors should be financially sound in their current state. What exactly does this mean? In order to be considered a lender, you need to reside within one of the States listed in the list of states that are part of the P2P lending platform, as well being able to meet the financial conditions for that state.

If you happen to reside elsewhere, you will need to meet certain standards to demonstrate that you are financially stable. In particular, you might be required to provide document proving your gross annual income. Based on which P2P lending platform you wish to join, you'll need to have a specific amount of cash for your annual gross earnings, and an asset worth at least the same amount. Your net worth usually includes your vehicle, home and other personal possessions.

Additionally, you need to get your identity confirmed. Investors must be legal that can be 18 or more in the majority of locations. Additionally, you must have your social security number. Organizations, companies as well as family trusts must be contacting the P2P lending platform you are hoping to be a part of to confirm your identity.

In terms of the investment minimums and the balance of the account the amount of investment and account minimums also depend on the lending platform you choose to join. In most cases they P2P lending platforms don't need a minimum balance for their investment accounts. But, it's a good idea to prepare in the event they decide to require an upper limit on their investment accounts in the near future.

If you are an investor you're permitted to invest whatever amount of money that you have. If, for instance, you put in $25 into an investment loan that is provided via the platform P2P for lending the investment of $2,500 lets you diversify your portfolio to up to 100 Notes. It is important to note the fact that diversification is about spreading investment funds equally across Notes that are linked to the borrowers, could yield dividends that are far more stable than the returns that are earned from one Note investments.

Styles, Investing Accounts, and Durations

P2P lending platforms typically offer an array of investment accounts, including personal accounts and joint accounts corporate accounts and minor or custodial accounts, as well as trust accounts. There are also rollover and retirement accounts.

Some investors opt to take an active approach that means they log into their accounts regularly then browse through the list of loans and then manually make their purchases. Some investors download the information of loans, so that they can conduct their own research prior to placing orders.

There are some investors who choose to select the investment criteria, and allow the automated investing capabilities provided by the lending platforms P2P carry out strategies to invest for them. This is why they can reduce time and energy but still have complete control over their investment.

In terms of the duration or time frame of your investment, you must be prepared to maintain your investment until their maturity. Some loans that are provided via P2P lending platforms come with at least 36 months of term of origination.

Investors generally need to wait for loans to be repaid which can take anywhere from up to five years or three months. It is possible to use P2P loans platforms, which enable you to access your money more quickly, however. In this case, for instance, you could create a secondary market which you can sell your investment and get access to your funds.

There are different P2P loans platforms, which demand longer tie-in time periods like up to five years, but they do not allow you to gain access to your funds. Naturally as an investor you'll need access to your own funds. You'd like to be able to access it easily and at any time you need.

How to access funds

Once you have successfully transferred the money to your account online You can then withdraw the money without having to pay any fees. This is one of the advantages with P2P lending. If you decide to change your decision at the last minute there is no need to pay any fees that aren't necessary. If however, the funds you have already transferred, you may be required to pay an administrative fee to terminate your loan contract.

The process of establishing loans

Although you don't typically have to handle the individual application and borrower but you'll have the chance to choose how much you would like to provide to others. Also you have complete control over the amount of money the borrowers have access to.

In the present the P2P lending platform that you choose is in charge of distributing and dispersing the funds. The funds comprise your own money as well as that of investors. They are given to those who have proved that they are worthy. The loan is made to various individuals in smaller amounts to spread the risk. For investors, you need to keep the money you loaned to you at all times so that you can earn profits continuously.

Redistributing Payments

People who have applied for loans, or those who borrowed are required to pay monthly. The payments must be in line of the conditions and terms of the loans they applied for. Being an investor you'll be able to receive a portion of the payments almost immediately. The money will be transferred directly to your account. In the event that this happens, you will have the option of withdrawing the money or use it for further borrowing.

As we mentioned before If you are looking to make money regularly the money you earn should be available constantly. Also, it is important to remember that the more quickly you redistribute your payments, the more quickly they'll also be to your advantage.

The internet is full of P2P loan platforms which allow investors to establish personal accounts. This means that their loan repayments are automatically transformed into loans. This is a fantastic option for those who wish to cut down on time and effort. They don't have to handle the whole process by themselves. They just have to watch for the payments to be made and their P2P loan platform takes the responsibility until they decide they would like to cash out the funds.

As an investor, laying at home and watching as your capital earn interest is exactly the kind of thing you would like to see happen. A lot of P2P lending platforms don't cost for these services except if the customer decides to withdraw the funds before being repaid by the lender. They provide the accounts for no cost and allow the investors to have more time to relax and also get the most out of their profits.

Investment Protection

If you are an investor or a lender as a lender, you want your funds to be safe and safe. Many P2P lending platforms hold reserves to cover the event of delayed payments do occur. They also have the capacity to handle any defaults triggered by the borrowers.

Furthermore there are some conditions, such as the funding of individuals being protected from their operating funds. This means that the money of the investor is used to lend and not used for anything else. In addition it is possible to find P2P loan platforms which provide security mechanisms. In particular, these platforms offer insurance policies that protect against the risk of loan defaults in the event the reserve funds are diminished.

Also the level of protection offered by many P2P lending platforms provide is so high that clients do not need to worry about their funds. The P2P loan platforms assessed the risks that could be associated with the borrowers. As the investor you are confident that your investment is safe and you'll get your money back.

Chapter 11: Investing Tips For Beginners

Now that you have a good understanding of the P2P loan, do believe that investing your money is a smart idea? If you're looking to be a lender, you have to prove you're capable of generating the funds. In the article you've read there are certain prerequisites to be fulfilled during the sign-up procedure. Before an P2P lending platform can accept members as members you must present all the necessary documentation and prove that you're an appropriate investor.

Typically having a net worth of $250,000 is sufficient to show that you have the financial capacity to be able to back the loans you provide. Also, if you earn an annual gross income of more than $70,000 then you're in good shape. If you earn this amount of money, you might be eligible as an investor. In most cases investors are required to contribute one percent of their earnings in P2P loans to the platform they belong to. Additionally, you must reside in the state where P2P lending is permitted.

Practical Tips for New Investors

You have the qualifications to become an investor. However, the process of getting started with P2P lending may be intimidating, particularly in the event that you've never attempted this before. A few investors are too enthusiastic and jump right into P2P lending, without contemplating their options. As a result, they are usually unhappy with the investment return. If you're looking to earn great profits through P2P lending, you need take into consideration certain elements. Here are some suggestions to assist you:

1. Auto plans or cherry-pick

The first thing you need to do will be to decide whether you want to make individual loans or choose an automated program provided through the lending platform you're working with. If you've got a massive amount of money you're willing to invest, then you might want to consider the automated option. A minimum of $10,000 could be considered to be a large amount. If you're looking to achieve higher than average returns, consider investing in individual loans.

2. Diversify

People who are brand first-time users of P2P lending must be diversified. Avoid making the mistake of placing all your eggs into one basket. If you can you should diversify your investments in the beginning between loans. It's best to diversify your investment portfolio as much as you can.

Lending Club and Prosper, for instance, permit the minimum investment of $25 per loan. Therefore, if your investment amount is $1000 you can divide it over forty loans. In the event that you've got a larger sum to be invested, then you may spend more than $25 as the minimum amount. However, make sure that no loan exceeds one percent of your investment portfolio.

3. Do not aim at the moon.

There is a common saying"Shoot for the moon" to ensure that if you miss it, you'll still be among the stars. However, this is not the best way to go about P2P lending.

If you have the chance to invest in loans that pay around 15 percent in interest. In addition, you have the chance to make investments in loans that earn greater than 20 percent interest. Between 15 and 20 percent, the latter appears to be the best option. Since 20 is larger than 15.

Although this may be true it is safer to choose the old method. If you are considering investing in P2P lending, you might prefer the option that comes with less risk. Because the higher interest rates can also translate to greater risks for the consumers. This is the group of people who typically have a high default rate.

If you are determined to invest in loans that yield 20percent, then you might not get the results you want. Instead of receiving your 20 percent, you could only receive 10 percent when you take into account all defaults that have happened.

As a beginner investor, you're better off with a portfolio with a broad selection of loan types. It doesn't matter what your level of risk-taking be. You are able to invest in grade A loans, however, it is possible to choose to go with grade B loans or lower, if it is a low-interest rate setting.

4. Use simple filters.

When you have transferred your money You may be able to come up with the thought of investing them in loans for individuals. This might prompt you to login to your lending account on P2P to go through the loans that are listed on the website. As you go through the list, checking out one loan after the other you realize that it can take you a long time to look through everything. It is possible to spend the whole day looking through loans. Therefore, it is important to reduce your options to a smaller size.

You must use filters. You need to sort your options so that you will reduce both time and effort. In this case, for instance, you could sort your options based on the quality of the loans. If you'd prefer to invest in loans of grade A and lower, you should eliminate loans that are grade B or lower. Also, if you want to invest in loans of grade B and lower, you should eliminate grade A as well as any other loans that aren't grade B.

Another information you can decide on is the number of inquires over the past six months. It is possible to look at the number of credit inquires the borrower made during the period. The information can be found in the credit reports that the borrower has. If you are someone who invests, you might consider investing in someone who doesn't shop around to obtain more credit.

It is also possible to use an option to filter out delinquencies. It is best to invest in a person that does not have a history of delinquency. But, it is important to keep in mind that a person's behavior in the past cannot necessarily guarantee returns in the near future. This method may not yield higher returns.

5. Examine the details of each loan.

You should take a lot of time reading about the particulars of loans you can find on the lender's P2P platform. For investors, you might prefer to stay clear of borrowers who didn't bother to give a clear explanation of their loans. It may also be beneficial to steer clear of borrowers who have not been able to answer the most basic questions of investors.

Of course, it is important to always take their advice with a pinch of salt. There is no need to question the authenticity of the borrower, but you shouldn't rule out the possibility that they might not be telling the all the truth.

6. Start gradually.

Investors who are new to investing tend to be enthusiastic about starting and doing the same things as experienced investors do. But, it is important not to get too excited. Don't make decisions until you've thought thoroughly. It's best that you've followed the guidelines mentioned earlier. At the point you begin investing your money, you'll already made a decision on your preferred options. You'll have determined the loan options by their grades as well as delinquencies and.

If you have $2000 to make your first investment, and you are considering 40 different loans. It is possible that you just have to make a $50 investment in each loan. But, this shouldn't be the situation. Instead, keep a variety of options. You should invest at least at least $25 per loan. You must invest less than the amount you've got now and put off a couple of weeks for a fresh group of loan to be posted on the online lending site. Once that time is over then you can go through similar steps and invest your funds in a variety of loans. You must be perseverant and disciplined.

7. Be sure to avoid taxation in any way you can.

The interest you earn on your investments are taxed at the normal rate of income tax and not at the more beneficial rate for dividends on stocks. Therefore, if you fall to the federal tax bracket of 28% bracket, you must pay 28% federal taxes on interest earned through P2P lending.

If you're looking to avoid problems tax-wise, you need invest your money into an

IRA. Lending Club and Prosper actually provide an IRA free of charge. You can join for the minimum of $5000 as your amount to invest. All of your earnings are tax-free.

There are many alternatives to pick from, like opening a brand new Traditional IRA, a SEP - IRA , a Roth IRA or even transferring your current retirement account.

8. Make sure you have an emergency fund for emergencies.

Before you deposit your funds in P2P lending, you must see to that you have sufficient money to cover your personal expenses as well as your investment. Be aware that once you loan your money to another and you aren't capable of getting it back until a certain period of time. If an unexpected event occurs and you aren't in a position to spend cash. If a member of your family is sick, or your home is damaged by fire or something unexpected occurs then you must be sure you are able to cover the cost.

What Happens If You Are a Student Loan Debtor?

If you've recently completed your college degree and are about to begin to look for your first job, you may be thinking that you're not capable of becoming an investor. This is not the case because even people just like you can turn into lenders and earn money through P2P lending. In fact, P2P lending can be an extremely profitable business.

However, even if you're technically competent to invest however, you must take a close look at yourself and the ability of your business to generate money. It is true that earning a profit through P2P lending is fairly straightforward, but you might have issues and difficulties when you're not cautious or have enough liquidity.

Imagine you're in the middle of a student loan credit that pays rate of 5. You would like to put your funds in a peer-to-peer lending platform which generally earns 9 percent return. In theory, it's possible to take home the spread of 4. Then, you can use the profits to pay off the credit card debt for your student loans.

But, it is important to be aware that there are the risks associated when you borrow money from P2P. In the end, it's an investment option that is not a substitute for it. Here are a few of the risks you need to be aware for:

* Borrower defaults. As you are aware P2P loans aren't secured. That means you as the lender don't have recourse if the person who took your money ceases to make payments. If the borrower doesn't have any collateral like a house or vehicle to secure the loan, there's no recourse in the event that the borrower defaults.

If your loans or funds are charged off The P2P lending platform will take the remainder of the balance on your account. Then, you'll be liable for the loss. Although the majority of P2P lenders have reserves funds, you must be prepared for the possibility of the possibility of a borrower's default.

* Bankruptcy. Sometimes, bankruptcy may be very sudden. In the event that you are in the event that the P2P lending platform you're working with fails you'll be liable for losses. This is the reason why you have be sure to research the P2P lending business prior to joining them.

The government regulations. Also, you must be prepared for any possible changes that be triggered by the government's regulations.

For instance, in December of 2015, a set of regulations was released from the Chinese government regarding lenders using P2P in China. For the United States, there are no regulations in place yet, however, you should be prepared for them in the event that they occur in the near future. If these changes do happen your investment could be affected in a variety of unpredictable ways.

Chapter 12: P2p Loans From The Borrower's View (Pov)

As a borrower you'll be required to complete an application form for the loan. However, unlike traditional credit applications your credit score won't be affected in any way. P2P loans are not able to have a significant impact on credit reports or credit scores.

If you're granted a loan, the rate of interest you get will depend on the duration of loan, the amount, credit utilization and credit history as well as credit score. Minimum credit scores required for a loan varies from one P2P lending service to the next. You must conduct the necessary research to discover how much the required credit score for the prospective P2P lending service is. It is usually at or above 600.

Furthermore, you need be aware that each state has their own laws and regulations in relation to investments and securities. This is the reason that investing and borrowing via P2P lending platforms isn't allowed in certain areas of the United States.

Some states don't allow P2P investment and allow borrowing through P2P. In contrast, there are states that don't permit P2P borrowing, however, they allow P2P investment. In other words when you are looking to borrow using Lending Club, the Lending Club P2P lending platform but you are not permitted to do so for Iowa, Nebraska, North Dakota, Maine, and Idaho. If you wish to make a loan through Prosper however, you won't be able to make it on the Prosper platform in Maine, North Dakota, and Iowa.

How Much Money You Can Borrow?

This is among the most frequently asked questions customers have to. Personal loans generally start from $1000 and go up to $35,000. If you're planning to begin your own small-scale business and require funding, you could apply for a loan of $15,ooo to up to $100,000. The amount isn't set however. It depends on the lending platform you sign up to.

Many borrowers take out loans through P2P lending in order to repay credit card loans or to refinance their existing loans. have. A small portion of borrowers borrow money through P2P lending to fund home improvements. The majority of loans are granted with a three-year or five-year duration. Additionally, it comes with monthly installments.

Why do Borrowers Choose P2P loans over other Loans?

The most significant benefit that P2P loans can offer to customers is the competitive interest rates. If you have excellent credit and credit score, you could benefit from an interest rate of 7percent. That's a fantastic deal. The percentage is less than other loan options, and is significantly lower than rate of interest for most credit cards.

The average national rate for P2P lending is around 13% but the rate you receive will depend on the lending platform that you sign up for. If the average borrower is carrying the debt of 20.7 percent interest rate, consolidating the debt might be a more economical option than signing up with an online lending platform.

In this regard that a person who is risky will also receive the highest interest rates. In this scenario P2P loans could be equivalent as traditional issuers of credit cards, as well as mortgage lenders. The lending options offered by P2P can be up to 25 percentage to 35 percent. If you wish to take advantage of the best rates of interest, you have to have a good credit score or loan quality. If you're a borrower with a Grade A rating, it means you're extremely financially sound and will not have any problems in getting your loan approval.

How long does it take to pay off loans?

P2P loans typically come with three-year or five-year term. They also offer monthly installments. Furthermore they're term-based, meaning that they're much more advantageous than traditional bank loans. If you are the borrower, you may think about making a move to P2P lending platforms first instead of going straight into the banks.

Peter Renton, the founder of LendAcademy.com that is an educational site for beginners to invest and borrow who are interested in P2P loaning, states there are those who approve of the concept of fixed terms for payment. He says that this type of payment can be used to enforce discipline for the borrowers. Because they know the time frame of their debts they will be prepared for the possibility of it. If you are aware that your loan needs to be paid back within three to five years, you'll be working hard to repay it.

Are there any hidden charges in the case?

Another question is frequently asked by borrower. As a borrower, you will certainly not want to be liable for any additional charges aside from the interest you are required to pay. But, the hidden costs are still dependent on the lending platform you're working with.

For instance, Lending Club charges a minimum of 1.11 per cent fee and the maximum amount of five percent fee for loans that are new. Prosper also has a minimum 1 percent fee and up to five percent fee for a loan that is new. What fee you are required to pay will depend on the amount of money you're able to borrow. The fee you pay initially is part of the annual percentage rate, and taken out of the balance of your loan prior to when you receive it.

You must be punctual in your payment. If you don't, you'll be charged higher fees. If you don't make payments on time, your charges will increase. For instance, Lending Club charges $15 for payments that bounce and 15% or $15 for payment made within 15 days from the date of due. P2P lending platforms do accept checks for payment. However, it is important to be aware that you will need to pay an additional $15 to cover the processing cost.

Tips for new Borrowers

If it's your first time transacting via P2P lending, be sure you get an idea of the process first. It is essential to comprehend the way transactions work as well as what to anticipate from them. Additionally, you need be aware that you should not get loans that are greater than the amount you require. Some people get caught up in the prospect of having more cash.

Remember that this isn't your money, and it has an interest rate.

Thus, only take out the amount you will need. As much as you can it is best to only take the amount you need so that you are not in a rush to ask for more. If you don't, it's just you who suffers at the end. If you are able to borrow excessive amounts of money, and you do not actually require it, you'll end in spending it on things that you do not really need like items like shoes, clothes such as a laptop, etc. It might be too late to discover that you've taken on a larger debt than you initially anticipated.

Additionally, you should only take out a loan that you know you are able to pay. You must be realistic when it comes to this. You should think about your work, salary and your the way you live. What do you do? It's steady? What amount of money do you earn during an hour or a day? If you take out a certain amount is it possible to pay it back within a specified duration of time? What type of life style do you lead? What is the amount you spend on rent, food and other necessities? Do you need to pay for school or for education? Do you have elderly parents or children to care for?

These are a few things you must consider before submitting for an loan. Don't let yourself be enticed by the possibility of getting additional funds since if you are unable to pay back your debt, you'll be in deeper financial problem at the end. According to the old cliche, you should spend only in the limits of your budget.

P2P lending could be more convenient as well as more flexible and cheaper than banks or other like financial institution. But, like the former, it could remain a challenge for those who are always in arrears with your payments. If you don't wish to endure a long time in debt, you should get your loan paid off within the shortest time possible. The quicker you are able to get out of financial debts, the quicker you'll be financially secure.

According to Renton According to Renton, it's more appropriate for those who are new to borrowing to take out loans with the shortest term. The reason is that the shorter the duration the lower the cost of interest. Renton says that the plan with a five-year term is the most appealing due to its lower monthly installments. However, it is important be aware that the interest rate is higher if you opt for loans that take up to five years before paying.

Another approach that you could consider. According to Renton it is possible to obtain a lower interest rate for your loan if you select the amount that is a less than a round number. For example, you might prefer to take out the amount of $4,995 rather than $5,000. The amount is almost identical however, the interest rates aren't actually.

Of course, you have to research the P2P lending service you are looking to get a loan from. A P2P loan is an excellent option to pay off all of your debts in one go. You can borrow the funds to pay off your debts, which includes student loans by borrowing funds from an investor through P2P. P2P lender platform. In addition, you must be aware of other options available.

Many credit institutions offer no-cost balance transfer options. Consolidation loans for debt are also appealing. Therefore, you might be interested in checking the rates offered by your local bank or credit union. If you're in need of more details about P2P lending, look up websites and other resources for free on the internet. It is also possible to download e-books on P2P lending.

Chapter 13: The Borrowing Guideline For Beginning Students

In the event that you're the one who is borrowing you must sell yourself. It is your responsibility to prove to investors that you're trustworthy. Also, you must prove that you're capable of repaying the money you have owed. If you follow these rules carefully, you'll discover that P2P loans are the most effective method to get loans.

Expert Advice to Borrowers from Investors

Everybody needs money and each borrower has his own reasons for borrowing money. There are people who need to borrow money in order to pay for school fees, and there are those who need to purchase a new theatre system in their homes. There are also borrowers that require money to start a business and there are those who have to settle their credit card debts in the shortest time possible.

Whatever the reason you are taking out loans it is important to know the workings of borrowing money in a P2P lending. Be aware that you're not competing with a few of other lenders. There are literally hundreds or even thousands of other borrowers looking to get an advance on these lending platforms. Therefore, you must present yourself as a professional to the lenders.

In the beginning, you must have a professional portfolio or profile. You must treat it as your application to an employment. Similar to your resume, you'll want your portfolio or profile to stand out and reflect your professionalism. It should highlight your most valuable assets, while concealing your weaknesses. You must make your first impression well otherwise the potential buyer will simply throw away your portfolio quickly and proceed to the next.

Keep in mind that certain investors utilize filters. If you do not wish to be excluded from the market it is essential to conduct your research about what investors typically want to see in a potential borrower. You've been reading about the needs of investors in a previous section of this book. This means that you need to offer them this information or, if you're not sure it isn't what you're about. It is essential to be authentic in your profile.

Beware of being a poor-rated Borrower

In P2P lending it has been observed that investors to spend on average seven seconds looking over the profile or portfolio of the borrower. In this brief time frame when they decide if they wish to give the borrower the chance to receive an loan and receive the amount he desires or deny the loan request.

Avoid being a poor-rated borrower to avoid being rejected. According to the investors one of the main reasons they are turned off is the inefficiency by the borrower. If they notice in the profiles or the portfolio that the borrower has is insufficient or is not backed by sufficient data or information, they ignore the issue and dismiss the profile.

Therefore, you must be patient and meticulously complete your profile. You must aim to be a grade A borrower. But, if you've previous records however, you are still able to do great and try to get to at minimum Grade B. Be sure to aren't a grade D or less. In the event that you are, lenders will be very reluctant to loan you money. It could be difficult to find someone willing to loan you money.

What is a Grade D (or lower) Borrower?

Your credit score is a testimony to your credit score. If you've had a record of 23 delinquencies within the last seven years, you'll be considered to be a the grade D. It's impossible to hide this fact. It is possible to look attractive by stating your job or earnings but you shouldn't think that investors will accept everything you claim. They believe that certain borrowers make up stories about their actual circumstances to be able to obtain the loan. Thus, the best method to maintain a positive profile is to keep an impeccable record. It is essential to have a great rating on your credit and history.

If you're a borrower with a Grade D rating is it too late to apply? Actually, not at all. Even though you stand a low chances of being granted an loan, you might still be able of proving yourself. How do you achieve this? You must be thorough in the description section. It is essential to explain the reason for your loan. Why do you need the money? What do you plan to do with it? What are the best ways to pay back the loan? Do your best to present yourself convincingly and convince an investor to be willing to risk their money on your.

In reality it is true that even those classed as Grade A or the Grade HR class of borrowers which have the lowest ratings, have an opportunity. This is due to the fact that they have extremely high rates of interest. Investors looking to earn lots of money could opt for high-risk borrowers. If you don't include any information in your profile, investors might think you're untrustworthy or incompetent, or perhaps not reliable in any way. If you've suffered from a negative experience in the past, and you want to improve your situation it is important to describe your reasons in the description section.

What is a Grade A Borrower?

Everyone loves Grade A students. Teachers favor students with straight A's, and film directors are more inclined to cast the actors or actresses that are top-of-the-line. A is after all the initial letter of the alphabet. If you're in the Section A category it means that you're among the most intelligent students. If you're an A-rated borrower this means you're among the top trustworthy loan borrowers. What is a Grade A borrower?

Someone who states in his profile as a borrower that he will pay back an amount of 6.7 percent interest on the loan is deemed to be to be a Grade A borrower. Why? This is because the interest rate is over three times that of the current risk-free ten year 1.9 percentage yield on Treasury bonds.

This individual could actually be "AA" classified since he is a great borrower. If he takes out a loan and pays it back quickly and at a reasonable interest. The borrower must also have an 800 credit score and over, doesn't have any outstanding debts, has an P2P lending platform score of at 9.5 and an average income rate of more than 25 percent, and who has a moderate to small amount of debt can also be considered an A-grade borrower.

Even if you're a good borrower and make punctual payments, you must remember to mention your position. Don't be embarrassed by your job because investors aren't interested in. It is possible to be medical doctor but when you have a poor credit history and cannot pay on time and make timely payments, you won't seem good to the eyes of lenders. Therefore, no matter what your position is, you must declare the same on your resume. Your credibility is important to investors, not the position you hold.

Also, ensure that you have proof to support your claims. For instance, if you stated in your personal profile that you pay in full and worked in the banking sector for a period of twenty years, and that's why you're a positive person toward money, you must be able to prove this. You may show receipts, or other relevant documents to serve as evidence. Certain investors are willing to make a bigger investment in those borrowers whose profile impresses them.

How to look good in Your Profile of a Borrower

Because investors don't necessarily know who you really are, and they are unable to see your profile, you must make sure you are as professional as possible on your online profile. This is the only method for them to meet your personality and know what you're about to say. It is important to use your profile to describe everything you want to be able to say in order for the investor to be convinced to approve the loan.

For this to occur, you must think like a loan lender. This is the initial thing you must complete. If you were in the position of the creditor, do you consider granting an amount to yourself? What characteristics would you like your loanee to exhibit? Sure, you don't wish for your hard-earned cash to disappear. Therefore, you must examine your own. Do you believe that you're in the right place to be considered a reliable and reliable borrower?

The most important thing investors need to be aware of is whether you are able to repay the amount you are owed. If you're able to pay, congratulations. You could be eligible for the loan. If it takes some period of time to pay back the loan, it's okay. In reality, the longer you pay back this loan the greater amount the lender earns. It is important that you are able to pay back the amount you borrowed. In addition, as it is you who was the lender you must pay back the loan as fast as you can so that you do not have to incur additional fees or more expensive interest rates.

You need to be honest on your profile, too. It is essential to disclose what you know about your lifestyle circumstances. You must state if you're working or are not. If you're employed, you must state your job title and other important information, for instance, what your earnings are. If you're unemployed it is important to be open about the fact. Also, you should inform the lender how you intend to pay back the money the investor will loan you.

It's also beneficial when you define your repayment strategy. It is possible to provide your investor all the details like how much you are able to allocate each week in order to make the monthly payments needed. It is also advisable to tell the investor about your life style to show him that you're accountable. If you only drinking and having fun and party, it will not reflect well when you present your resume. If your earnings is not that great but you're extremely practical in your lifestyle, you might be able to convince an person who is investing in you that you are accountable enough to make payments on time and make monthly payment.

It is essential to be as explicit and as clear as you can. Don't be shy about the reason for the loan. If you require funds to cover the cost of your tuition and so on, you must state this. You should not just state on your profile that you require the cash so that you can look forward to an excellent future. It is essential to state clearly that you are in need of the money since the enrollment deadline is in the next few weeks.

It's also fine even if your motives aren't so urgent or noble. For instance, if you want to take out a loan in order to get an eye lift or some implants for your breasts, you must remain honest and state that in your profile. The investors will not care about how you spend the cash so long as you are able to repay it. There is no reason to fabricate a story or exaggerate the facts. Be honest about your intentions. If you attempt to conceal the truth, you'll just appear as untrustworthy, and investors won't be able to grant you the loan that you need.

Before you send in the application form, ensure that you read the form and double-check it for grammatical and spelling mistakes. Also, make sure that you used correct punctuation marks. It's easy to believe that these issues don't have any significance however they could affect a significant amount on investors. If you're not punctually correct and grammar, prospective investors might be turned off. They may conclude that you're not serious about your application since you didn't make the effort to find errors. There's no need that you be flawless. It is enough to be honest and genuine. Otherwise, you could appear as a fraud.

Be sure to are also able to state your expectations on your profile. Tell the investor what you hope to gain from the deal. For instance, if you have a great credit score and earn an adequate monthly income then you should inform your investor you are hoping to be able to conduct a smooth transaction between you. You could inform him that you required borrowing money this time due to an emergency situation, but you is confident that you are able to repay the loan and will pay the loan back.

However If you have 580 credit scores and you earn $35,000 a year, it might be too high to qualify for an amount of $25,000. This is only logical. What can you do to repay that amount within the shortest amount of time when your annual earnings are only $10,000 off of the amount? Certain P2P lending platforms determine the Debt to Income ratio of the borrower before they send out request for loan. This allows them to determine how much they are able to comfortably take out. If you are able to borrow more than you can repay the loan, you could end up becoming an default lender, which isn't good for anyone who is part of the lending system of P2P.

Also, ensure that you don't look insecure when you post your picture. It is important to assert yourself to convince an investor to loan the money. But, you must not beg or come to appear desperate. If an investor thinks you are in desperate need they may conclude that you're weak and you don't have what is required to repay the loan. However when you appear with confidence, then the lender might conclude that you are competent and are competent to repay the loan.

Respecting the terms of the contract

Since this is a business transaction it is expected that you are presented with the form of a contract. In the contract, the amount you are borrowing and the time frame by which you are required to repay the money are stated. There are other specifics that will be examined at the close of this chapter.

If you take out a loan you must respect whomever lends you money. This person was the one who helped you in your time in times of need. So, it's only right to follow the terms of your contract and stick to your promise to pay back the amount you have owed.

Investors place their faith in the borrowers. They assist them in improving their financial situation. In the event that you fall behind in your repayments and fail to pay the amount you owe, you'll disappoint as well as hurting your investor the person who, despite every circumstance, took a an opportunity on you to help you. Don't be that kind of person who refuses to let other people away due to selfish motives. You must become a responsible lender.

The lending market of peer-to-peer is where second chances usually are made. It is the place where those who are struggling financially turn to. People needing money get help from those who can help them. If you do not make the payments on time then your credit rating is at risk because of your inability to repay your loan will affect your score on credit.

As a result, you'll not be able to be eligible for loans in the near future, and also obtain an apartment, a car or even an employment. Credit scores are important as it's what banks, employers and other organizations take into consideration when you approach them.

What can you expect to see in the P2P Lending Contract?

The details that both of you negotiated on are in the contract. This document serves as evidence of the transaction. The contract you receive will be contingent of the P2P lending business which you work with , as well as the lender.

The following are a few of the most often encountered components of a P2P lending contract:

Definitions. These are the common phrases and terms that are used in the entire contract. Examples:

* Borrower. It refers to an legal entity or an individual who is registered and accepted by the P2P lending firm to become a borrower.

* Business day. It refers to a day that falls on the day of the week or a day that bank is open to business.

"Client Money Account. It is the bank account where your funds deposited are kept for you so that you can request loans.

* Default event. It is the inability of the borrower to keep through with the payments or conform to the conditions and terms in the agreement.

* Information. This refers to information that can be downloaded or viewed from the P2P lending site. It can include price information and policies, images, and even reports.

• Information Technology. It is the term used to describe hardware for computers, like telecom equipment and networks software for computers, databases owned by or leased by the P2P lending firm.

* Lender member. It refers to the individual who has registered and was accepted by P2P lending platform to become an official member.

* The loan agreement. It provides details about the loan sought by the lender.

* A loan commitment. It refers to a legally binding commitment made by the lender towards the lending platform of P2P.

* Repayment. This refers to payments to the loanee in accordance with the terms of loan agreements.

The repayment of loans. The loan repayment agreement states that the borrower is required to pay the loan back each month in amounts that the lender and the borrower have agreed on. The repayments the borrower is required to pay must include fees for opening as well as interest and account maintenance fees and principal repayments that are not paid, as well as any other charges for additional services.

The interest on loans. The borrower's obligation to pay the interest for his loan begins at the time the loan is deposited into his bank account. The rate of interest is based on the amount the borrower and lender have agreed on.

Funding and closing of loans. The borrower can submit an application for a loan on the website that is owned by the lending firm. The loan will be looked at by the investors associated with the P2P lending business. They can commit to different amounts.

Failure to pay. If the debt owed by the lender to the borrower is less than of a month past due and still unpaid or repaid, the lender or his representative have the right to demand repayment, which may include the payment of interest and fees and within a specific duration. If the borrower is in default on his obligations, he will be subject to certain penalties.

The collection and reporting of delinquent loans. If the borrower hasn't paid back his loan within the timeframe agreed upon or after 30 days have expired, the P2P lending platform is entitled to file a complaint against the borrower with the consumer reporting agencies.

Obligation of the borrower to give details. Prior to the borrower being granted credit, he must to give accurate and factual details, including details of contact and address.

Notifications. Any communications between two parties can be sent to the lending company P2P. The majority of notifications are accepted as valid if they are stored within the databases of the P2P lending platform regardless of whether recipients have actually read them.

Other obligations of the borrower. The borrower is required to be able to provide misleading, deceptive or false representations on his application or lie about his identity. Additionally, he must acknowledge that he will never accept or provide any item which isn't within the agreement, and other conditions.

Chapter 14: Peer-To-Peer Lending: What Is It And How It Can Benefit You

Before you can learn how to earn money from peer-to-peer lending, we must first know what peer-to-peer lending is:

In peer-to-peer lending is where investors (the investor) provide money directly to private individuals or businesses via the internet via a platform. Peer-to peer lending may also be called "market space", "person-to-person" or "P2P" lending. Popular peer-to peer lending sites are Lending Club, Prosper, and Zopa.

In essence, P2P lending companies remove financial intermediaries such as banks and credit unions because they eliminate the middlemen between buyers and sellers - they can help lower the cost of borrowing for the borrower, and boost the investment return.

Through P2P, you will get steady interest rates for time periods as short as 30 days to five years when you put your money into loans using P2P platforms. This opens the possibility of a new method of investing passively.

P2P is also increasing in popularity particularly with those who are looking for greater returns than the stock market can provide. In addition, they have having more control over their investments as opposed to the stock market.

The University Cambridge's Centre for Alternative Finance estimates that in the UK more than $8.06bn was lent to individuals and businesses in the year 2016.

The advantages of P2P lending

P2P lending can yield higher returns for the investor, while also lowering the rate of interest for the borrower. One of the major benefits of P2P lending include:

Increased returns: As mentioned earlier P2P lending can provide you with more yields from your investments. Although the bank is offering less than 1% returns and stock market returns range from 10% to 2%, P2P loans could yield as high as 30 percent!

Allows you to diversify risk: When you lend through P2P you can join other investors who have much smaller loans in $25 or increments of $50. Additionally, you are able to diversify your risk over many different credit cards for consumers rather than just investing in one loan. You can invest in a portfolio consisting of hundreds or even thousands of loans. You may also opt to invest in grade A loans, where all of your borrowers have an excellent credit histories. You can also opt to higher risk loans with high interest or mix high risk or low risk loan into your investment.

* You have the option of choosing your lender P2P lending lets you work with various categories of borrowers on your network. It also guarantees that your borrower's identification verification. The borrowers have the chance to learn about the loan's interest rates, terms and conditions and other factors that are related to the financing algorithm, and the credit score that a borrower must have to qualify for the loan. Additionally, you are able to invest in loan that is best suited to your needs. Knowing who you're lending money to and the reasons for which they

require the funds, you can gain an assurance of security.

* P2P lending gives you the chance to meet other investors, exchange experiences, and get any details about lending. It is also possible to debate the proposed P2P lender policies and decide on guidelines that will help you make your investment more secure.

In the end investing with P2P lending is easy and consistent, as well as providing the highest level of social accountability. How did P2P lending come to be an investment opportunity that is so attractive?

Background Of Peer To Peer Lending

P2P lending is an innovative concept born of the rapid trend in the social sphere, as well as the expansion of crucial businesses and technological advancements. Today, the majority of people are growing frustrated with the rigid demands of traditional financial institutions and are opting to run their business, such as social lending. But the most interesting part is that the concept of social lending isn't necessarily a new idea.

The concept of social lending has been in existence prior to the time that money was first invented hundreds decades ago. The evidence that has been documented shows that the first social lending occurred in the early 1700s, as Jonathan Swift (the famous Irish author of Gulliver's Travels) loaned small amounts of money to people in need . He also demanded no charges for the repayment.

The social lending method was by far the most sought-after money lending technique in Europe during in the late 18th and 19th century. The rise of the influence of banks during the 20th century made the social loan less popular. However, the rise of the Internet has revolutionized the entire idea of social borrowing.

The year 2005 was the time that the first P2P online lender, Zopa, was launched in the U.K. Till now; Zopa claims to be the top-ranked firm on the U.K. market. In the same way, P2P operations were pioneered by Prosper in the U.S in the year 2006. In the first nine months of operation, Prosper financed about $20 million in loans and had built up a membership of 100,000 members. Prosper was monopolized until the introduction of Lending Club in May 2007. Lending Club was launched majorly as an Facebook application, but then became an individual website competing with Prosper just a few months after.

Between 2008 and 2009 the two companies Lending Prosper and Lending Club Prosper didn't allow new cash to come in from investors (they had a few days of "quiet intervals") due to they were regulated by the Securities and Exchange Commission (SEC) requested the two companies Lending Club along with Prosper have all loans posted through their websites as promissory note with the federal government. Presently, the financials of both firms are available to the general public, since the notes are all registered with the SEC.

After a break from the "quiet times" Both Lending Club and Prosper began to pay greater focus on managing risk. The reason for this is that prior loans from 2006-2007 were not able to meet expectations of investors due to the high rate of default that led to losses of capital. For example, Prosper's loan default rates were 40 percent between 2006 and 2007 whereas the default rate for Lending Club during the same period was approximately 24 percent.

With a greater emphasis on managing risk, investors received higher returns, and default rates were reduced significantly. For instance, Prosper estimates default rates for loans that were issued in 2009-2010 at 5%, while Lending Club's estimates run around 4percent.

Each Prosper as well as Lending Club have also enhanced the appeal of their lending through P2P by the introduction of new "products" recently. For example, Lending Club offers small business loans to investors that have been selected and , when it comes to consumer loans, you are able to take advantage of three or five-year loans with each of Prosper along with Lending Club.

P2P lending in the U.S is expanding at an extremely fast rate. The two platforms Prosper as well as Lending Club are experiencing growth at a very high rate, and the total of both of loans issued recently surpassing $15 billion of total loans granted. What are the factors that are behind this huge increase in the P2P lending market?

P2P lending works in accordance with such terms as:

* The desire to enjoy your own freedom, coupled with social activismthat allows you to feel that you're in control of your investment.

The advancement of technology has led to the decentralization of virtually everything. This means that you're likely be unable to reach the traditional banks to place your money, when you are able to effortlessly and quickly make it happen regardless of where you are.

The Web continues to expand in helping to facilitate "mass co-operation". In turn, you are able to be part of a group of friends and join online in large groups to accomplish the same objectives. For instance, your constant interactions with your fellow members on Facebook might cause you to create diverse investment strategies to increase the value of your friendship.

While it is true that you can get impressive returns from P2P lending, it's crucial to remember that this kind of investment comes with its own set of challenges that you must be aware of in order to overcome them.

P2P Lending Challenges

Before investing on P2P loan, it is important be aware of these points:

There is a risk of losing the entire amount you invested. If, for instance, you choose to take a risky loan due to the high-interest rates they pay You will increase the chance of losing your investment. So, even though higher interest rates might seem appealing, it is essential to be aware of the risks associated with these rates.

To mitigate these risk, you're better off investing in smaller loans (like $25 per day) particularly if you're just beginning to get started. This is because you are able to afford losing $25 instead of losing $1,000.

* New industry regulations: Since P2P lending is also a relatively new industry, you're likely to encounter waves of lender consolidation,

administrative/interface changes and even alterations to the lending practices. Therefore, it's important that you stay current with these details.

In order to help you reduce the risk of taking a risk with P2P lending, it is important to be aware of the way P2P lending operates.

How to Get Started with Peer-to-Peer Lending

As we have mentioned before, P2P lending services function as matchmakers online by offering an online platform that lets those with money to lend or invest can meet people who want to borrow, though it's not physically. In essence, a lending platform is a firm that transfers your funds to vetted lenders. That is you do not invest in the P2P platform, but rather the P2P platform merely allows you to connect with a potential borrower. The P2P platform functions as an intermediary. It earns its income through charging a proportion of the loan fees to you as well as your customers.

P2P platforms operate to function as "cupids for investment" by bringing together investors and borrowers investors and matching them in accordance with the diverse set of rules and guidelines, including the rate of the loan, the borrower's risk profile , and the term for the loan. If you sign up to the P2P Platform, you have the chance to be included in a group of individuals lenders that can join forces and offer loans. You could, for instance, be part of a consortium of 100 lenders and use your funds to one loan. It is possible to invest just $25 in every loan, or as high as $1000.

Getting Started

1. In the first place, you need to sign up on an P2P lender's website (For this instance, we have selected Lending Club) by signing up. Create the account for investment.

The sign-up process is easy. Simply fill the application form giving your usual information like your name as well as your social security number and address. Remember:

The state you reside in is extremely crucial. This is due to the fact that P2P isn't accessible to certain states like Texas as well as Ohio.

* Open a regular or retirement account. Regular or taxable accounts require a different application process than retirement accounts, such as the Roth IRA. It's easy for people to become into something similar to an IRA after they've been involved with this asset by using a regular account.

2. Then, you can utilize your password and email address to login to your account. After that you will be able to view your "account overview" screen, which is shown below. You can click"bank account" or "bank account" link to connect to your bank.

3. Prepare to add funds to invest by linking with your banking account. Once you're to the "bank account" page, you can connect your checking or savings account with the Lending Club. Click the "transfer" link and transfer the amount you wish to trade in your Lending Club account.

Think about investing at least $2,000 to be able diversify into 80 A-grade notes with lower risk ($2k is equivalent to the value of 80 notes at $25 each). If you're considering making an investment in a trial period across all grades the transfer of at least $5,000 would be necessary. This means you'll be able to diversify your portfolio across the entire risk spectrum. In essence, you'll have 200+ notes each worth $25. For beginners, you should stick to the $2000

4. You can now begin investing $25 in A-grade or higher notes. Click"Browse Notes" and click on the "Browse Notes" link to see an extensive list of loans. The goal is to put $25 notes in 80 of the loans available.

5. If you click on"Rate" in the "Rate" column, then sort the loans available in order to obtain A-grade loans. From here you'll look up the most secure A-grade loans. They are usually displayed in dark blue colors. If you click on the dropdown menu and choosing 250 loans, you'll be able to view the loans that you are able to think about. Select 80 of these A-grade notes and then click the "Add to cart" button.

6. You can look up your order by visiting"View order" on the "View your order" page.

7. When you are confident in the information you see If you're satisfied with the

information displayed, click "Continue" to go on to"Place Order" screen "Place orders" screen.

8. Click"Place order "Place order" button to deposit your funds into the loan you've chosen.

It is possible that you will not be able to find the entire amount of loans you're looking for. For example, A-grade loans might not be available when you apply. Consider logging back in later.

* The loans are provided with different descriptions like their profile as a applicant, their credit history, etc.

The good news is that many P2P loan platforms (like Lending Club) filter loans before allowing users to invest, particularly A-grade loans. In this particular instance, Lending Club considers all its A-grade loans as secure, with a very low risk and it is able to guarantee steady yields.

In time, you might be looking to increase your return by filtering the loans you have invested with different conditions in order to get a slight performance increase. For instance, you could decide to only loan to those who have a high annual incomes or other appropriate criteria based on your specific needs.

It is also essential, for a newbie to learn about particulars on loans to acquire the class of asset, the borrower and to connect with others. This might not result in higher returns but, as the expression says, "knowledge is power!"

9. With $5,000 in your account, you could invest in a variety of grades, around 200 notes. This could include the more secure A-grade loans and the more risky G-grade loans. Make sure to diversify your portfolio with 200 notes, regardless of how big your notes are. Diversification will help you to make your capital more receptive and also keep your income steady in the event that one loan shows an insignificant performance.

10. When you trade with P2P loan platforms keep in mind your objectives of engagement. You're looking to increase your earnings. This is why reinvesting your profits is crucial. Within 30 days of fully making your initial

investment then you'll start receiving the payments of your borrowers. The payments will show as cash on your account. You can invest the money into additional notes using:

* Making a few times during the month and then putting your money into A-grade loans.

* Enable "automated investing" But, your account must be running at an investment minimum of $2,500. All your money should be invested in A-grade loans.

* You can click the "Transfer" button to transfer payments into your bank account to put into investing somewhere elsewhere. It's essential to keep your cash balance at a minimum.

Normally, your money produces income when it is given out. Therefore, if your capital gains and interest aren't put into a fund, your return diminishes as your cash ends at a point of sitting in your account to lend over a long period of time. Think about reinvesting your profits into loans that meet your interest as soon as you can.

These steps could be applied if you opt to invest your funds through Prosper or another P2P lending platform. To ensure that you are safe regardless of the platform you choose, you must try to learn the rules that govern these platforms and your investment on the internet. Once you're confident investing in safe loans and loans, you're able to move into the more risky loans to increase your overall return.

It is crucial to note that to earn excellent returns, you have be cautious when choosing the type that P2P platform you invest on. In the next chapter we will be able to learn more about the various P2P platforms you can invest in and the best way to select the best one based on your needs financially.

P2P Lending Platforms

Generally, P2P lending platforms concentrate on specific kinds of borrowers, and thus loans tend to move in the same direction. But, based on the lending platform you select to invest on you'll have access to various loans that you can choose to invest your money depending on your needs.

There are websites which are solely focused on lending to private people as opposed to those that focus on those who work for themselves as well as property developers and smaller businesses, or even providing loans for commercial property owners and others. Additionally, some sites might consider the value of an organization's outstanding invoices prior to deciding whether or not to lend. Here are a few more ways that individual P2P lending platforms differentiate themselves:

Some sites allow anyone can apply to be a loaner however, other sites only work with people with high net worth with a minimum amount of money might be required from you prior to investing in them. For example, Lending Club in addition to being a company that operates in just 36 states, it also requires investors to earn an annual gross income in excess of $70,000 or a net worth of more than $250,000. In contrast, Prosper operates in 36 States only. States with different residents may have different requirements , too.

The process of assessing credit scores can be carried out largely online by various platforms. However, you might meet those who prefer to meet with borrowers in person and visit their offices, and review the business strategies and their accounts.

* You could be able to find sites which offer fixed-rate deals. This is where you are required to enter into a loan commitment with a fixed rate and your offer is considered based on first-come-first-served.

Other websites also have in competitive "reverse auctions" that allow you to compete against other lenders by offering to loan at the lowest rate of interest. For instance, you can accept a rate of 9% over your rival's 9.5 percent; thus winning the bid. Additionally, other platforms might go further and establish the minimum rate to the level at which competitive rates aren't allowed to drop.

* You can also pick individuals as borrowers on certain platforms. This is not the case with other platforms and instead, they will simply transfer your money to borrowers , without you having any involvement.

* Some platforms can make loans complete and allow you to purchase the finished portion of the loan from them. Others, however, may choose to matchmakers and connect you with potential lenders.

There are also the possibility of coming on platforms that are managed by financial experts who are experienced or former bankers. While others could be simply tech experts who have no experience in banking at all.

The way in which P2P lending platforms operate will give you an idea of the degree of trust you can place on any specific platform. In particular, a platform that is run by experts in the field is more likely to be reliable since the owners have a sense of authority in the industry. So, it is essential to conduct some background checks prior to selecting a specific lending platform.

How do you pick the best investment platform to make investments with? The following elements should guide your choice on the platform you choose:

* The type of borrower that you want to lend money to as mentioned previously some platforms might prefer to lend to specific types of particular borrowers. So, it's your decision to select one based on the type of borrower you want to lend money to. For instance, would the lenders you choose to lend money to small businesses or small-sized businesses? Do you consider a customer's annual earnings essential before you offer them the loan? These and other questions will influence your choice on the lending platform that you select.

* How can you protect yourself from losses? Do you provide any type of security? A few of the security practices implemented by different platforms to reduce the chance of losing your money include:

a. Provision funds: A site for lending through P2P could have a reserve of funds that can be used to cover any defaults.

b. Asset security: In cases where your borrowers grant an obligation over tangible assets , such as property or collateral. In this scenario the collateral will be sold to repay the amount of debt.

3. P2P lending sites could have strict lending criteria in particular the lending platform could go through extensive due diligence before making it possible to take part in a specific loan.

d. Diversification of loans In this instance the platform permits you to divide the loan between multiple lenders to lower the chance of sustaining a default.

* Review the information that has been published about the P2P lending website. Learn about the history and the history of this site. For instance, how many instances of default have been uncovered? Are the investors' funds recuperated? Or , what steps were implemented to ensure that the investor's funds?

The staff running the website should have abilities and expertise in evaluating the creditworthiness of your borrower and lending funds? It is crucial that the P2P lending service you choose those who are able to pay back your loan. This is a crucial aspect, especially if the prospective P2P lending service doesn't contemplate investing all of their own funds into loans.

• Does this P2P lending system have a back-up mechanism in place? What is the outcome in the event that the P2P platform is not functioning? Most P2P sites have contingency plans in place to ensure they will close any new lending and also have the control of the loan book transferred to another business. Always make sure you check backup agreements between the potential P2P lending website as well as other companies to ensure that the current loan book will continue to be maintained even if the P2P lending site ceases trading. If you have a similar agreement in place, your will not be affected even if the P2P lending platform is not able to function.

Incorporating the above tips in mind will help you select a P2P lending site that you can trust to reap great rewards. After you've found the right P2P lending platform and you're ready to move on and invest your cash.

The next chapters will offer an array of amazing strategies to be successful in the world of peer-to peer lending and make high-quality returns.

Peer-To-Peer Lending Investment Tips

If you have met the criteria to become the first investor to a certain P2P lending website You must devise an effective plan of action in order to safeguard your interest. These suggestions are an easy and sensible plan can be used to create the best P2P lending experience:

1. Determine if the plan is an automated program or not. If you're planning to put aside large sums such as $10,000 You can begin by implementing an automated plan. Like Lending Club's PRIME feature was specifically designed to offer you an entirely hands-off approach. This feature is designed to allow you to reinvest your earnings when you're paid.

2. Diversification is essential, especially for a brand new P2P lender. Be sure to exceed the minimum investment only if your capital is substantial. If not, you can take advantage of

this cap and make as numerous loans as you can. Make sure that no loan exceeds 1percent of your P2P portfolio of investments. It is possible to diversify your loan portfolio by a variety of methods such as:

* By investing in various risk grades: You can invest across the entire credit spectrum by purchasing notes of various risk grade

Take into consideration different regions as the different regions perform differently in terms of economic. So, you're more likely to get more benefit from a location with a greater performance, and offset it by balancing it out with a less performing region. But, you should not run the danger of excessively diversifying.

3. The loan you make should be consistent. Do not just make one lump amount! You could put in an amount in one lump to invest when borrowers are not as numerous, consequently, this could affect the rate of interest you get when you invest your money. It is best that you spread out your money out so you can take advantage of the good times,

and even when there are times of trouble it won't impact your investment as significantly.

4. Make sure to use the filters that are simple to use on the P2P lending website for the purpose of not having to spend a long time looking through loan requests individually. Prosper comes with a powerful filtering system that will allow you to process your loan requests the loan requests as quickly as you can. But, Lending Club is a somewhat undeveloped. You will must obtain the CSV file which contains the loans available and then make use of Excel to sort the loans.

P2P lending sites like those like Nickel Steamroller can also help you filter. Use filters such like:

"Inquiries*" is the amount of inquiries your prospective borrower has conducted over the past six months. It is more secure to invest in someone who is not looking for credit in many other sources.

* No delinquencies in the past can affect your return on investment from previous loans. But, don't rely on your past performance as a guarantee for future returns.

5. Learn the specifics of each loan to understand the different kinds of borrowers. Be sure that the borrower has specific descriptions of the loan and tries to answer all of your inquiries as thoroughly as is possible. Keep in mind that you might not be able to get all the information you need from a lender.

6. Begin slow: You might be eager to put in as much as you can. But this is not recommended since you are only beginning to learn about P2P lending. It is best to begin by investing the least amount the site will allow. After a while, and after you feel confident you are able to invest additional money.

7. Reduce your tax bill If your investment with Prosper and Lending Club earns interest, the interest is taxed at a the standard tax rate. For example the fact that you're in the federal 28% tax bracket, all the P2P lending-related interest will be taxed at that same rate of 28 percent rate. This is an enormous burden! It is best to invest into an IRA to reduce the burden. There is a tax-free IRA through Prosper and Lending Club, however a minimum of $5,000 is required, however,

interest earned is not subject to tax. Additionally you can roll over your current retirement account or opening an entirely new Roth IRA/Traditional IRA or a SEP-IRA may help in getting rid of tax. In the absence of tax in the first place, you'll get a more harmonious balance between liquidation and taxation.

8. Split your money across two lending websites. This is a different method of diversifying your investment portfolio, however, it requires totally two distinct platforms.

9. Be sure to commit to lending for a specific time frame and then set goals based on this timeframe. This is crucial since it helps you avoid making rash choices because in the bottom of your head you are aware of objectives that you must attain within a certain timeframe.

It is vital to keep in mind that, in order to maximize the returns from a P2P lending platform, you must be sure to avoid losses as much as you can. Keep in mind that P2P lending investments aren't like shares that will surely increase in value. Therefore, focusing on limiting the amount you invest in loans that do not pay back will reduce the risk and increase your return.

Conclusion

Thank you for buying this book!

I hope that this book was helpful in helping you understand everything you need about peer-to peer lending to enable you to begin making investments or borrowing.

Next step would be to begin investing your money and earning profits if you wish to become an investor. Or begin applying for a loan and benefitting of the lower interest rate if plan to be a loanee.

Thanks and best of luck!